YOLANDA E

CAREERS IN ANIMAL

LAW

WELFARE, PROTECTION, AND ADVOCACY

Cover design by RIPE Creative, Inc.

Printed in the United States of America.

15 14 13 5 4 3 2

Library of Congress Cataloging-in-Publication Data

Eisenstein, Yolanda.
Careers in animal law / Yolanda Eisenstein.
p. cm.
Includes bibliographical references and index.
ISBN 978-1-61632-961-7
1. Cause lawyers—United States. 2. Animal rights activists—United States.
3. Animal welfare—Law and legislation—United States. I. Title.
KF299.A55E37 2011
346.7304'6954023—dc23

2011027959

Discounts are available for books ordered in bulk. Special consideration is given to state bars, CLE programs, and other bar-related organizations. Inquire at Book Publishing, American Bar Association, 321 N. Clark Street, Chicago, Illinois 60654.

www.ShopABA.org

Contents

About the Author

Yolanda Eisenstein is a lawyer with an animal law practice, the Eisenstein Law Office, in Dallas, Texas. She is an adjunct professor in animal law at SMU Dedman School of Law. She is active in the State Bar of Texas Animal Law Section and the ABA Tort Trial and Insurance Practice Section Animal Law Committee, where she serves as vice chair. She volunteers with various animal welfare groups, including the Texas Humane Legislation Network, an organization dedicated to the passage of pro-animal legislation in Texas. She writes and speaks at conferences around the country on animal law and animal protection issues.

Yolanda graduated with honors from SMU Dedman School of Law. She is licensed to practice law in Texas and New Mexico. Prior to starting her own animal law practice, Yolanda was legal director for an international human rights organization where she represented asylum seekers, victims of international human trafficking, and victims of domestic violence.

Acknowledgments

I specifically want to thank the following people for their expertise and insight on the book: Sarah Babcock, Ethan Eddy, David Favre, Patti Gearhart Turner, Chris Green, and Fran Ortiz.

Many thanks to my friends and colleagues, especially Don Feare and Randy Turner, who have generously shared their knowledge and advice; and to all of the advocates who work on behalf of animals. A special note of gratitude goes to my parents who taught me the value of human and non-human animals.

And thank you to my husband, Abram, who encouraged me to go to law school in order to make a difference in the lives of others and has supported me in all of my endeavors, animal and otherwise.

The Animal Lawyers

There are many lawyers working in animal protection. I have included profiles of a small number of them. I hope their stories inspire and motivate you. While statistics abound indicating that many lawyers are unhappy in the work they do, you will not find those lawyers in this book. They are passionate and driven, and all enjoy the work they do and find it meaningful. They exemplify the belief that working in an area that allows you to pursue a passion is the essence of a satisfying career.

As I talked with these lawyers I began to see certain shared characteristics, although their jobs varied. In developing their careers they were proactive; they never sat back and waited for something to come along. They networked and many created their own opportunities, often in areas that did not previously exist. No one fell into the perfect job.

They all work hard, and that dedication does not end at five o'clock. They believe in the law's power to make a difference, and their commitment to animals extends beyond their law practice—they write, they speak, they teach, and they volunteer. And they have a sense of humor—while serious about the issues, you will see from the "milkshake-loving barbequer" that animal lawyers do not take themselves too seriously.

Following are the lawyers who generously shared their stories. I want to personally thank them for their time and their commitment to making the world a better place for animals, and consequently, all of us better humans.

David Favre
James F. Gesualdi
Adam Karp
Jonathan Lovvorn
Ian A. Robertson
Belinda Smith
Senfronia Thompson
Joyce Tischler
Randy Turner
Ledy Van Kavage
Bruce Wagman
Michelle Welch
David J. Wolfson

Introduction

This is the first book about careers in animal law, a milestone in the development of an exciting and relatively new area of the law. Animal law is still evolving, giving you the opportunity to directly participate in that evolution, follow a passion, and create your own job. Animal law is not an ordinary practice and this book is not an ordinary career guide. Beyond legal jobs, it is a book about animals, meaningful work, and the law; and how to combine them to build a rewarding career.

What constitutes animal law is far from settled. Some lawyers are unfamiliar with this new field or view it as a practice only related to companion animals. I hope to increase awareness and broaden the perceptions about animal law. The reality is that the law touches all animals—farm animals, wildlife, sea life, and companion animals.

My goals in writing this book are to introduce you to animal law, help you assess whether it may be the right career path for you, and provide you with information on a variety of opportunities, legal and nonlegal.

Is This Book for You?

This book is for people who care about the welfare of animals. It is for lawyers and law students who are interested in careers where they can use the law to protect or improve the lives of animals. It is for lawyers who want to work for clients—whether corporations, governments, individuals, or nonprofits—whose work involves animals guided by a concern for their welfare. In my research and interviews, this reality quickly became clear, as the lawyers who called themselves animal lawyers were animal protection lawyers. And those seeking to practice had no interest in pursuing jobs they considered harmful to animals.

Jobs generally fall into three categories, as far as animal protection is concerned: (1) those clearly focused on animal protection; (2) those in the grey area, where the jobs and/or opinions may vary; and (3) those that do not involve animal protection. In a job in the first category, the lawyer is actively working in an animal protection role. For example, a staff attorney with the Humane Society of the United States has a job in animal protection. The organization's mission is clear and its activities in support of animal welfare are transparent. The job seeker does not have to look far to learn whether he or she will be working as an animal lawyer in the area of animal protection.

In the grey area are those careers that involve animals, but the animal protection factor is not so clear (or is controversial). For example, there are some animal advocates who believe that keeping animals in zoos is always wrong and that all zoos should be abolished. Other advocates believe that zoos are acceptable if the animals are treated humanely and given appropriate environments. Is the lawyer for the zoo, whose goal is to help the zoo care for its animals, an animal protection lawyer? It depends on your attitude about zoos. You get the picture.

Finally, there are certain industries whose practices lack transparency and have been exposed for animal cruelty and abuses; jobs in such industries are not considered animal protection jobs.

The jobs in this book are in the first two categories. Rather than make a personal judgment on "grey-area" jobs, I have included them with the thought that you, the job seeker, can do the necessary research to form your own opinion, and decide whether a certain career is right for you. I have not included jobs in the third category, which entail situations that are widely considered inhumane for animals.

How to Use This Book

In an effort to be as comprehensive and creative as possible, I have included jobs, companies, and organizations that have close connections to animals, as well as some with more tenuous connections. Other animal-related jobs exist that are not in this book, with some yet to be created. So think of this book as an idea and strategy book. Read with a pen and highlighter in hand, and make notes that spark ideas. Keep your mind open to all possibilities, whether you are looking to change careers, promote animal welfare, or find your first legal job out of law school.

The book offers a number of different approaches. You can choose legal areas of interest or focus on your passion for certain animals, and then think about how you can expand on those areas. You can see how your past experience and education can increase your opportunities. You can also look for careers by industry or position.

The Internet is a great investigative tool and you should use it and other available resources to learn more about the animals, companies, and organizations in the book, as I have merely scratched the surface. Couple your technological research with personal contacts. The animal law community is friendly and still relatively small, making it easy to find and meet people. I echo the advice of many of the lawyers I interviewed in strongly advising anyone who is interested in working in the field of animal law to meet the lawyers who work in this area. It is the best way to learn more about animal law and the lawyers who practice it. There is no substitute for face-to-face contact.

How I Got Started

1

I have a solo practice in animal law in Dallas, Texas. I am an animal protection lawyer in that I only take cases that I feel benefit the animal's interests as well as the client's. I represent clients in traditional cases such as dangerous dog hearings, contract disputes, nonprofit issues, and estate planning.

When I started my practice in 2007, I was the only lawyer in Dallas who called herself an "animal lawyer." I knew that launching a solo practice, especially in animal law, would not be an immediately profitable venture, but my desire to work in the area of animal protection motivated me to make the effort. All other aspects of a solo animal law practice fit within my goals and lifestyle. I am a self-starter, an independent worker, and like to have control over my schedule. I love animals and have always been fascinated and intrigued by them. A law practice focused on helping animals was a perfect fit.

Before starting my practice, I researched the market and found there were other lawyers in Texas who, while not full-time animal lawyers, had been handling cases for years and working in animal welfare. They provided me with valuable information on the types of cases I would have and some of the benefits and challenges in working in animal law. More importantly, they became friends and allies and valuable resources in animals and the law as I developed my practice.

I read everything I could find on starting a solo law firm, avoiding malpractice, animal law, and animal protection. If you are thinking of starting a practice I advise you to do the same. I also volunteered my time with a number of nonprofit animal welfare organizations. They are always happy to have lawyers on their boards and committees.

When I opened my practice, I had developed a professional website and stationery package, and set up all of the systems I needed to handle clients.

I then turned to marketing my practice and networking. I had a marketing and public relations background, which came in handy. My marketing expertise plus my "new and different" practice in animal law paid off and generated a number of articles in local media, bar journals, and animal publications. People read the articles, which contributed greatly to the initial growth of my practice. While I have never specifically tracked the source of my clients, I do know that referrals are a significant source of business and that my website generates a number of inquiries, in and outside of Texas.

My practice continues to evolve. While I still work with clients, I spend a significant amount of time in other animal-related endeavors. I enjoy teaching animal law at SMU Dedman School of Law, working with the ABA Tort Trial and Insurance Practice Animal Law Committee, and volunteering with the State Bar of Texas Animal Law Section. I volunteer and speak regularly on animal law issues and participate in the legislative process with the Texas Humane Legislation Network. Through animal law, I have created my perfect career through a law practice, volunteer work, speaking, and teaching.

Life's opportunities are sometimes the result of factors that are out of our control, such as timing, market forces, and coincidence. However, careers are also made through planning, networking, and hard work. In my situation, and in those of the lawyers I interviewed, planning, networking, and hard work played a far greater role than luck or timing.

Our Relationship with Animals

2

Before moving into a discussion of animals, careers, and the law, a brief history of our relationship with animals is in order. The evolution of that relationship is important and has contributed much to the recent development of the field of animal law.

Humans have had a long and varied relationship with (and dependence upon) animals, and that relationship continues to evolve. In our agricultural past we relied on animals for food, labor, and transportation. Cows, goats, chickens, and pigs provided milk, eggs, and meat. Oxen pulled plows in the fields and horses pulled the wagons that transported people from faraway homesteads and farms to town for buying and selling goods. Dogs kept on the farm were used for hunting and protection from wild animals that might stray upon the property or attack the livestock.

We still use animals for food, but the industrial age brought technological advances that forever changed the farming industry and our relationship with animals. Tractors replaced oxen for plowing the fields and trucks replaced horses as a means of transporting people and goods. Animals used for food seldom live with us, and most of us rarely see them in their natural states. We buy meat from animals that have been slaughtered and carved, conveniently out of our sight, into neat family-sized portions in cellophane-wrapped packaging. Pasteurized milk is delivered in cartons, and eggs sit on refrigerated shelves in plastic containers with individual compartments to prevent breakage. The look of the meat we eat has little resemblance to the animals it came from, and most consumers have little interest in knowing how that transformation occurs.

More recent technological and operational changes in the production of animals used for food have created Concentrated Animal Feeding Operations (CAFOs), which have drastically changed the farming industry. This production method relies on densely populated confines, intense feeding, and rapid growth for mass production and quick turnarounds to market. While CAFOs have allegedly given us cheap and plentiful meat, reports of animal suffering, exposés of worker abuses, environmental problems, and health and sanitation issues make the true cost more elusive.

Many Americans today have never been on a farm or spent any time with farm animals other than perhaps at a state fair. However, companion animals play vital roles in the lives of many people. Changes in our society have resulted in fewer extended families that live together or in close proximity, which provided companionship and emotional support to parents and grandparents as they grew older. While financial support may be there, physical proximity is not, due to our transient and mobile society. A child may live 2,000 miles away from a parent, making it more difficult to provide the physical comfort and support available to families that live in the same house or even in the same city. Moreover, with job transfers and divorces, many people find themselves alone. Consequently, people from all walks of life have turned to companion animals, mainly dogs and cats, to help fill the gaps left by absent humans.

One indication of society's high regard for its companion animals is that many people consider them family members, celebrating birthdays and taking them on vacations. And if you haven't noticed, the phrase "companion animal" is replacing the word "pet" as a term more reflective of our relationship with and respect for animals. Some states have gone so far as to use the term "guardian" rather than "owner" when referring to animal ownership. Estimates vary, but some reports have put our expenses for food, toys, clothes, and veterinary care for our "pets" at more than $35 billion a year.

The sad side of the story is that our desire to have animals in our lives sometimes outweighs our rational thinking. Many owners too often fail to consider the responsibilities that accompany caring for an animal. Shelters are overflowing with dogs and cats that people abandon, often for trivial reasons. In the United States, we euthanize an estimated 5 to 7 million unwanted animals a year, despite the efforts of thousands of rescue groups and shelters around the country working constantly to find homes for healthy animals.

Our fascination with animals does not stop with dogs and cats. We purchase exotic animals as pets, and wild animals continue to captivate us, especially as we learn about their intelligence. One need only spend a small amount of time at a zoo or aquarium to see the fascination on the faces of children and adults alike. Wild game hunting, zoos, aquariums, circuses, and wild animal sanctuaries all exist because of that fascination. However, as scientific evidence grows of the highly developed intelligence and social structures of creatures such as dolphins, elephants, and gorillas, many have begun to question our right to use them for no other reason than our entertainment. And regrettably, we have hunted many wild animals to the brink of extinction in the name of recreation or to acquire trophies, jewelry, furniture, or purported aphrodisiacs.

Throughout history, the legal aspect of our relationship with animals has remained unchanged. All of the animals in our world are defined as "property." That status controls virtually all aspects of our relationship with them. Property status determines ownership rights, valuation, and damages when animals are involved in legal actions. Every job in animal law will be affected in some way by an animal's legal status as property. While most lawyers agree that all property is not equal and that a dog is not the same as a chair, opinions vary widely as to whether the property status is a positive or negative designation and what should be done about it. And unfortunately, the failure to build consensus around a viable alternative means that many state animal laws have remain unchanged and unchallenged, some dating back to the nineteenth century. These outdated laws and cases place constraints on animal lawyers who are trying cases in a twenty-first century society.

Animal Law Today

3

What Is Animal Law?

We have a long legal history with animals. In the United States, cases involving animals date back to the seventeenth century. Most lawyers still remember the 1805 *Pierson v. Post* case from law school about the ownership of a wild fox. So, animal law and its practitioners have been around for many years. However, history's version is not today's concept of animal law, although we are still saddled with some of its archaic laws. The contemporary practice of animal law has emerged, in large part, from the activities in the late 1970s of a group of lawyers who organized with the specific intent of using the law to provide greater protection for animals. Joyce Tischler, who is profiled in this book, is one of those lawyers. The creation of the Animal Legal Defense Fund and the efforts of Joyce and her colleagues contributed greatly to the scholarship and case law that comprise the field of animal law today. Their activities instructed other lawyers and organizations in putting the law to greater use in animal protection.

Perceptions exist that animal law is the same as animal rights, a social justice movement. Although it started with the animal protection movement, animal law is a legal discipline. It is the law that affects, but not always protects, animals. While definitions vary somewhat, the first animal law casebook provides a good working definition: "statutory and decisional law in which the nature—legal, social, biological—of nonhuman animals is an important factor . . .".[1] Animal law is a city ordinance, a state or federal law, an international treaty, or a case whose provisions or result has an impact on an animal or animals. It is law, legal precedent, rules, and regulations that affect animals' care and use, how they can and cannot be treated, and even whether or not they are considered animals.

To be sure, animal law incorporates various cultural and philosophical ideologies of the animal rights, civil rights, and environmental protection movements; this is one feature that makes the study and practice of animal law fascinating. The scientific research on the intelligence of animals, the accelerated extinction of certain species, changes in farming practices, and ethical views of society all contribute to the body of knowledge that comprises animal law. All of these factors, some of which are reflected in the brief history in this book, provide a glimpse of why there has been growth and interest in the field of animal law.

The Growth of Animal Law

In 2010 the Animal Legal Defense Fund reported that 121 law schools in the United States and Canada offer a class or classes in animal law. This statistic reflects how far animal law has come since the first casebook was published ten years ago. When law schools initially began offering animal law classes, students enrolled more out of curiosity than an expectation of making animal law a career. Now, however, professors see a greater number of students who are interested in practicing animal law and seek out law schools specifically because of their relevant curriculum. In addi-

---

[1]Bruce A. Wagman, Sonia S. Waisman, & Pamela D. Frasch, Animal Law: Cases and Materials xxxi (4th ed., Carolina Academic Press 2010).

tion, more lawyers are looking to incorporate animal cases into their existing practices or start solo firms.

The legal profession has also acknowledged the growth of animal law. The ABA Tort Trial and Insurance Practice Section has an Animal Law Committee. State and local bar associations have formed animal law sections and committees and are holding conferences. In its January 2008 "What's Hot and What's Not in the Legal Profession" issue, the ABA *Law Practice Management Magazine* listed animal law as a "hot" niche area of practice. A search of "animal law" in the *ABA Journal* listed forty-two stories in 2009.

Heightened interest and professional recognition notwithstanding, the traditional animal protection legal jobs—animal cruelty prosecutor, staff attorney for a humane organization, and animal law specialty practices—exist, but have not kept pace with demand. Much work remains to be done to develop the field of practice. Part of that work is to expand the perceived scope of animal law from small companion animal practices to include the legal work involving all animals and the various legal disciplines it encompasses.

The following are examples of the cases and legal issues that comprise animal law:

- Animal cruelty
- Animal fighting
- Animal protestors and free speech
- Animals in entertainment
- Animals used for food
- Animals used in scientific research
- Conservation issues related to wildlife and habitat
- Constitutional issues related to animal law
- Consumer fraud and deception in the sale, trade, or lease of animals
- Contracts for the sale, use, lease, or trade of animals
- Custody of animals in divorces
- Dangerous dog hearings and other violations of local laws and ordinances
- Dog bites
- Equine law

- Federal enforcement of animal protection laws
- Hunting
- Intellectual property
- International trade
- Local ordinances and state laws
- Legal consulting related to animals
- Ownership disputes
- Pet trusts and emergency planning
- Service animals and the Americans with Disabilities Act and Fair Housing Act
- Veterinary malpractice
- Wrongful death or injury of an animal by public or private entities

The preceding list is by no means exclusive; it is merely a start in describing what reflects a broad area of the law. The lawyers who deal with these issues may do so in a law firm setting, a corporate office, a government agency, or a private practice.

Getting Started

4

A Personal Assessment

A first step in any career decision is to take time to think before you act. Assess your personality and take stock of your knowledge, experience, needs, and interests. Set goals. While you may confirm what you already know, you may also discover something new.

The following questions are based on interviews with other lawyers, talks with students, and personal career decisions. Some questions are general in nature, but they are designed to help you determine whether animal law is a good (or practical) fit, and what type of job you should pursue. Go through the list and keep your answers in mind as you read the rest of the book. Also consider enlisting the help of friends and family in your assessment. You should find their insight helpful, and maybe find some of their answers surprising.

As you read the jobs and career profiles that follow, you will see how the answers to these questions will be helpful.

- Why do you want to practice animal law? What is it about the *animal* that attracts you? What is it about the *law*?

- What skills, education, and experience can you add to your legal expertise? What sets you apart and will enhance your skills in the practice of animal law? Do you have a science background? Do you have a history of volunteering? Are you good with numbers? Do not leave anything out. While not required, these personal "extras" are often overlooked or discounted, but can enhance your marketability and help you narrow your focus.
- How much money do you need to make? How much do you want to make? How important is it to you? Do you have other financial resources? Will you have student loans to repay? Family obligations? These are important questions, and the answers will greatly impact your career decisions in both the short and long term. Nonprofit jobs may be fulfilling, but salaries are generally lower.
- Do you like a job with structure and hands-on management feedback, or can you get career satisfaction through personal successes?
- Is it important that your efforts have a direct impact on animal welfare or will you be content to work in an area where the impact is more indirect, unknown, or long term?
- How hard do you want to work? How important is leisure/family time?
- How well do you handle stress? Certain jobs carry more stress than others. Do you thrive on it, or does it hamper your ability to be productive?
- How flexible are you? Do you have a spouse and children? Can you pack up and go to Kenya to work in conservation for a year?
- Are you an extrovert or an introvert? Your need to socialize and interact with others is an important factor in determining whether you would be happier in a collaborative situation or in a "solo" scenario.
- Are you a litigator or do you want to litigate? Many animal law careers involve litigation. Is being in a courtroom appealing and stimulating? While some cases are won, others may not go in your favor. Are you good at enjoying the wins and handling the losses and moving on?

- Can you emotionally deal witl
ecuting animal cruelty cases (
scenes of abused animals. Hov
the realities of animal abuse?

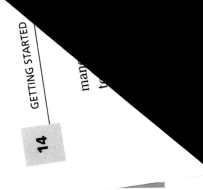

For Law Students

Master the Basics

Law students often ask what they can do to prepare for a career in animal law. The most important credential for any job once you graduate is to have a solid, broad-based knowledge of the law. You have heard this before, but a strong foundation in the basics is particularly essential in animal law because it touches virtually every area of law. Animal law is complex, and without a solid foundation you will not get far in animal law or any legal career.

Beyond the Basics

Consider the following activities to enhance your knowledge, learn more about animal law, bolster your resume, and make friends with the key players who can assist you:

- If your law school doesn't teach animal law, organize students and lobby the faculty and administration to add it to the curriculum.
- Take classes such as administrative law, natural resources, environmental law, criminal procedure, and First Amendment that will give you a well-rounded legal background and relevant education for an animal law practice.
- Talk with your animal law professor or lawyers working in the field for advice based on your interests.
- Participate in family, criminal, and human rights clinics to gain hands-on advocacy and court experience.
- If your school has a Student Animal Legal Defense Fund (SALDF) chapter, join it and be an active member. SALDF is the student organization of the Animal Legal Defense Fund (**www.aldf.org**), a national nonprofit organization dedicated to fighting animal cruelty and promoting more hu-

treatment of animals. Your participation can be a topic of conversation in interviews and highlight your interest in the subject.

- If your school does not have an SALDF chapter, start one and remain involved. (In 2010, there were 146 SALDF chapters represented in United States law schools. ALDF has information on its website to guide you through the steps to start a chapter.)
- Go to court and sit in on animal-related cases. In some jurisdictions judges are specifically assigned to hear these cases. If not, contact the city prosecutors who handle the animal cases. They should be able to provide you with information on cases and the judges who hear them. They may even invite you to accompany them to a hearing, which will give you a close-up view of animal law.
- Learn about animal-related legislation. Find out what your city and state are doing regarding animals. Look for animal lobbying groups and volunteer. When in session, spend a day at your state capitol talking to legislators and legislative aides about animal bills that are being considered.
- Monitor the news about animals. Virtually every day there are local, national, or international news stories about animals and animal welfare. Reading these stories will help stimulate your thinking about possible careers and may even lead to a job opportunity. Keep clippings of these articles to use when you write papers and when you start your job search.
- Develop an animal law resume (in addition to your traditional resume) that includes volunteer work and other credentials absent from your basic resume. It will be ready with minor edits if an opportunity arises.
- Look for seminars and independent study projects that will allow you to write papers on animal-related issues. Animal law touches virtually every aspect of the law, so this should be easy. These papers will give you a writing sample involving both animal law and a traditional area of the law, such as contracts. They will provide potential employers with an example of your writing skills and highlight your

legal thinking in both a traditional area and in one that is still relatively new. If you are a 1L, approach your legal research and writing professor and ask him or her to include an animal law issue as one of your assignments.

- Research and compete in moot court and writing competitions. The National Animal Law Competitions are presented every February by the Center for Animal Law Studies at Lewis & Clark and hosted by the Harvard Law School Student Animal Legal Defense Fund. Competition includes legislative drafting and lobbying, closing argument, and appellate moot court. Registration typically opens in September. For more information, visit **www.NationalAnimalLawCompetitions.org**.
- Look for opportunities to publish your papers in animal law journals. There are several around the country, and most take student articles. Research what has been published and choose to write on a new issue or present a twist on an issue that has already been examined. As a new field, animal law gives you a better chance at publication than an established area.
- Talk to your career counselors and professors about animal law jobs. Do not assume they will not be helpful.
- If your school requires charitable hours to graduate, ask to have animal welfare nonprofits added to the volunteer opportunities to fulfill those hours.

Networking

When you are looking for a job, trying to raise money, or meet someone, everyone tells you to "network." The concept and the word itself are so overused that most people don't even think about what it means. We vaguely realize its importance when life and career are going well, then wish we had worked on it more diligently when we are looking for a job or donations to our nonprofit. It is difficult to create an "instant network" when we need it.

Simply put, a network is a broad-based group of contacts—friends, acquaintances, and business associates—who know you and like you. Start with your current friends, associates, and family, then add to that network a group of new people who can open up business opportunities. It takes time to meet people and build relationships, which is why it is a good idea to start in law school. People must get to know you before they will help you. The way they get to know you is through networking, which entails meeting at conferences and events, having lunch, and volunteering.

If you are not an outgoing person, networking may be difficult, but the benefits should convince you to move past your fears. The following are a few suggestions to get your animal law network started.

- Identify the people and lawyers in your area who are involved in animal law issues. Do not rule out professors, who are often overlooked but can be valuable resources. Contact them and, to the extent possible, meet with them. Humane organizations, shelters, nonprofits, city and state commissions and task forces on animals, and prosecutors are places to start. It's important just to know who these people are.
- Join professional organizations that can connect you with key people when you graduate and look for a job. The people in leadership positions are usually master networkers. Most organizations give law students a discount, making it easier to participate as a student than as a new lawyer working to pay back student loans. Legal organizations such as the ABA Tort Trial and Insurance Practice Section Animal Law Committee and the animal law section of your state or local bar association (if established) provide excellent inroads into the field and contacts with lawyers. (In Dallas, for example, the young lawyers association has an animal welfare committee.) Once you have joined, attend meetings and get involved. Lawyers will not get to know you if they never see you.
- Attend conferences and events related to your interests. There are increasing numbers of animal law conferences and animal-related workshops and conferences. Once there, network. Introduce yourself to speakers and other attendees and indicate your interest in an animal law career. Many lawyers will, in turn, introduce you to other attendees and offer advice on your future practice.

- Talk with the district attorney's office. Learn who is prosecuting animal cruelty cases and talk with him or her about the job. If internships are available, as they often are, apply.
- Volunteer, to the extent possible, while in law school and when you graduate. Animal rescue groups, legislative groups, farms, shelters, and zoos all offer distinct views of animal welfare. You will learn the personalities of the people who work in various aspects of animal protection. Not only will this experience provide contacts and possible job opportunities, but it will also help you decide if animal law is the right career path for you.

Advice on networking would not be complete without a comment on social networking. The twenty-first century has spawned online ways to network; that is, to establish and cultivate relationships without seeing anyone face-to-face. There are numerous social networking sites for people with interests ranging from starting a business to knitting.

While technology has made communication easier, email and text messages and even business-oriented social networks have not yet replaced personal contacts in the context of finding a job. You may have a great Facebook page, and employers do look at them. But if I am going to introduce you to my friends and business contacts, I want to know who you are, which still means personal interaction. As humans we still assess each other through body language, eye contact, and face-to-face conversations. Obviously, personal meetings are not always possible, but online networking will rarely be sufficient until a person gets to know you. Once a relationship is established, online communications are appropriate and a convenient way to stay in touch. You can also stay informed of what is happening in the social groups you've established.

Monitor the Market

The employment market changes, sometimes quickly. Factors such as economics, competition, technology, international events, and politics impact the overall market and the types and number of jobs available. In law, the lines continue to blur between what constitutes the official practice of law and the unauthorized practice of law. People appear *pro se*, handle their own divorces, and write their own wills and contracts. Businesses take certain services in-house to be handled by non-lawyers.

Like the general market, employment opportunities in animal law are affected by these same factors and can change quickly, making it important to monitor the events that affect animals. The passing of new laws, formation of nonprofits and foundations, and changes in existing animal-related organizations can all impact the job market. Parties on both sides of the animal welfare issue are actively litigating and pursuing legislative changes at the local, state, and federal levels. When new laws are enacted, such as when a state passes a commercial breeder law, new jobs may open up, including legal ones. The astute job seeker will be current on legislative issues, conservation activities, and general animal-oriented news at the local and national levels.

While in law school, keep your finger on the pulse of the legal job market for the obvious reasons, but *also* stay current on events in the animal welfare community. Make it a point to know the people who make the news and the events that will affect the animal law environment when you graduate.

For Lawyers

Almost anywhere you look today, you read news of lawyers who are unhappy with their jobs. Stress, overwork, negative public image, and disillusionment with the practice of law are troubling issues that may lead to depression and substance abuse. Ethical lapses, and what some view as an increasing lack of civility by some lawyers, have damaged the image of the legal profession to the extent that some have left altogether. These issues are naturally of concern to lawyers and the professional organizations that support them. The ABA and state and local bar groups recognize the problem and have developed lawyer assistance programs for alcohol abuse, drug addiction, and depression.

For other lawyers, the situation is not so dire, but the legal profession may no longer meet their expectations, the work may not be fulfilling, or they may simply have the feeling that it is time to move on.

If you are thinking that it may be time to change direction or reinvent your career, I hope this book will give you confidence along with some ideas. Read the career profiles to learn how other lawyers have expanded, changed, or reinvented their practices. Some of them started over completely, deciding on law school after an entirely different career. These lawyers had families, debts, and other obligations that most of us bring up as excuses when we think about making a change. The reality is that our families want us to be happy and will work to make it happen.

Be sure to review the questions in the Personal Assessment section at the beginning of this chapter. If you have not given any thought lately to where you are personally and professionally, it is a good time to revisit your skills and goals.

We know there are unhappy lawyers, but where are the happy lawyers? You will find them in this book. While writing about careers in animal law, I made an important discovery. The lawyers profiled in this book are happy and satisfied with their careers. Time and again in interviews they expressed how stimulated and energized they are by the work they do. So what's going on? Some of the reasons are obvious. They have found an area of the law that has meaning for them. They set career goals and met them. They have a sense of belonging. They are part of a group of lawyers who are working together to fight the injustice they see in the way animals are treated.

The important role of law in fighting injustice is too often forgotten or discounted. It is the reason many of us went to law school. The lawyers in this book remind us that personal fulfillment in the practice of law is not necessarily about money, prestige, or winning. They may not be paid high salaries, are not likely to find themselves on the list of Who's Who in the legal profession, and may lose as many cases as they win. But they know the work they do makes a difference and is paving the way for greater animal protection.

If you are not happy, there is no time like the present to rethink and reengineer your career and join the happy lawyers.

Becoming an Animal Lawyer

5

Follow the Law

By now you have learned that animal law is a complex field and incorporates numerous areas of the law. One approach when deciding how to pursue an animal law career or adding animal law to your practice is to choose by area of law. Start with your current areas of expertise or those that interest you and see how animal law fits into your set of skills. Once you focus on the law, you can then choose an animal or species that interests you, or target specific industries or law firms.

The following are brief summaries of key areas of the law that are relevant to animal law. It is not an exhaustive list, and you will no doubt think of other fields that intersect animal law.

Administrative Law

Administrative law deals with the federal and state agencies that administer and manage the laws passed by Congress and the states. In animal law, the work of federal agencies such as the Animal and Plant Health Inspection Service (APHIS), which is responsible for the Animal Welfare Act, plays a significant role in the interpretation, implementation, and enforcement of the law. With approximately 100 federal animal-related laws to oversee, agency work is significant. It is easy to see how expertise in administrative law is a valuable asset to the animal lawyer, particularly those who work with federal law issues.

Constitutional Law

Constitutional law is central to animal law on a number of fronts. Property rights, religious practices, illegal search and seizure, and due process are examples of constitutional issues that arise in animal law cases. Lawyers defend the rights of animal welfare protestors, challenge city ordinances and state laws, and sue government entities for wrongful acts related to animals.

In addition, laws that affect animals, in positive and negative ways, continue to be passed at federal and state levels and must pass constitutional muster. These laws are scrutinized carefully by stakeholders on both sides of the issue and challenged if weaknesses are found. The lawyer who is well versed in constitutional law and the administrative and regulatory framework is in demand as these issues are played out in the courts.

Contracts

For the lawyer who does not want to be involved in litigation, the development and interpretation of contracts is relevant in areas of the law regarding the sale and use of animals. Rescue groups, humane organizations, breeders, veterinarians, and other organizations and companies that conduct business related to animals work with contracts. Also, the federal government hires lawyers specifically for contract work. (See "Working for the Government" in this chapter.)

Criminal Law

Criminal laws related to animals are investigated and prosecuted at every level of government. Municipalities and states have criminal laws against animal cruelty, animal fighting, and dangerous dogs. The federal government enforces criminal laws related to violations of federal laws such as the Endangered Species Act, dog fighting, and animal abuse.

Environmental Law

Environmental law is a combination of federal and state statutes (plus common law) that is intended to protect the country's natural resources and the environment—the air, water, plants, land, and certain species of animals. Animal law overlaps with environmental law when actions affect animals, such as the destruction of habitats. Before the existence of animal law in law schools, students took environmental law if they were interested in animal welfare. Now, a curriculum in animal law may include environmental law, administrative law, First Amendment, and trial advocacy.

Many see the development of environmental law and the challenges it has faced as relevant to animal law's evolution today. It has matured and grown to the point that several other related fields have emerged, including natural resources law, land use law, energy law, and international environmental law. Natural resources law is narrowly focused on natural resources—land, air, water, and other resources—controlled by the United States government. Land use law is specific to the zoning and regulation of land by local, state, and federal governments. Energy law concerns regulation of the energy sector. International environmental law includes the negotiation of and compliance with international treaties related to the conservation and preservation of shared natural resources, such as the air and the oceans.

Family Law

Animals are considered a part of many families today. The fact that these "family members" are paradoxically classified as property under the law creates dilemmas in family courts. Litigants fight over custody and judges grapple with the emotional aspect of such cases, coupled with legal issues related to ownership, visitation, and best interests. Family lawyers are well advised to know the issues and the law and include animal custody in their areas of expertise.

Intellectual Property

Intellectual property law includes copyright, patent, and trademark law, as well as laws related to trade secrets, licensing, and unfair competition. Intellectual property is relevant in animal law in that patent law protects new inventions and discoveries, including animals. Trade secret law also comes into play where a patented discovery can be protected as a company's trade secret.

The Harvard Mouse, an "oncomouse" with a genetic susceptibility to cancer, was the first multicellular organism to be patented in 1988. While the idea of patenting an animal was shocking to some at the time, the patent was granted; other living entities have since been patented. As science and technology advance, cloned, genetically altered, and transgenic animals occupy center stage at the national and international levels. Animal lawyers with expertise in intellectual property and ethics will work through the legal and ethical issues affecting businesses and society.

International Law

International law is generally divided into two areas: public international law, which governs the relations between countries, and private international law, which governs relations between private entities. Expertise in either area involves animal law. In the public arena, states in the United States and other countries are passing humane legislation regarding the treatment of animals and setting standards in agriculture that may conflict with international treaties and trade agreements. As an example, at the time of publication of this book, issues are being played out on the international stage as Canada and Norway fight the European Union on its ban of seal products. Also, Japan's whaling activities have long been the subject of controversy, and in June 2010, Australia instituted proceedings against Japan in the International Court of Justice, alleging that Japan breached its international obligations through its whaling in the Antarctic. On the agricultural front, genetically modified foods and animal cloning are creating international trade disputes and debates as some countries refuse to accept altered or cloned food. Most recently, California's passage of new standards for the treatment of farm animals is reverberating internationally. Private companies that sell on the international market will be looking to the courts and settlement organizations to resolve the disagreements. These are examples of uniquely international animal law issues, and the lawyer who knows both international and animal law will be front and center as these controversies heat up.

In the United States, many federal statutes have international implications. Existing treaties will continue to be reviewed and discussed and new treaties will be negotiated as situations change. Lawyers with expertise in administrative law, litigation, legislation, criminal law, and international law will have valuable skills to market. China and South Africa are examples of two countries that are in the process of drafting animal welfare legislation and have looked to animal law experts in the United States for guidance. For those lawyers with a desire to play on the international stage, this is an area to consider.

The field of international law is as broad as animal law itself. Animal law encompasses the legal management of Kenya's wildlife parks; contracts for the sale and trade in exotic animals and the purchase of wild animals for zoos; the continued protection of endangered species, including policing and prosecuting illegal smuggling; the establishment and management of wildlife sanctuaries and nonprofits; the purchase and legal protection of animals for scientific research; and the preservation of the world's ocean life. There are jobs based in the United States that are international in scope, and there are jobs based internationally for those who want to live abroad.

The following profile describes a multifaceted, international animal lawyer. You will see in the following story that a concern for animal welfare, knowledge of the law, and a head for business not only work together, but succeed.

Career Profile

Ian A. Robertson, Barrister and Solicitor, Veterinarian, Entrepreneur
Auckland, New Zealand

An entrepreneur is synonymous with a capitalist, a person who sets up a business and assumes the associated risks in the interest of making money from that venture. In the past, a lawyer would not likely consider himself an entrepreneur or her law firm a business. Business was anathema to a learned profession such as the law. Historically, the law was considered a profession, distinct from a business, and the lawyer's work was viewed not merely as a job but a "higher calling." Even today, it is business schools, not law schools, that teach business acumen and entrepreneurship. However, times have changed and competition is intense. Law firms have evolved over the years, and in order to compete have combined the professional status of law with the practical reality of needing to be creative, be competitive, and operate effectively as a business to be profitable. The individual lawyer must do the same.

Ian Robertson is a New Zealander whose titles and talents include barrister and solicitor, businessman, consultant, educator, entrepreneur, and media personality. While somewhat defying description, his career can best be categorized as animal law on an international scale. His career reflects his life-long interest in and enjoyment of animals, learning, and risk-taking, which he has channeled into a business that helps animals and, yes, makes money.

Ian's career involves a lot of international travel, but he spends most of his time in Auckland, New Zealand, a country whose position on animal welfare has played a role in his success. New Zealand still depends heavily on production animals (animals farmed for food or fiber, including cattle, sheep, goats, poultry, deer, and pigs) for its economic growth and well-being. More than half of the country's gross domestic product comes from production animals; it has been stated that New Zealand's standard of living relies more on production animals than any other developed country in the world.

While the country uses animals for commercial purposes, its people are serious about animal welfare. The willful ill treatment of an animal can result in a penalty of $100,000 and a prison sentence of five years for an individual, and a fine of up to $500,000 for a corporation. The court has the power to confiscate animals and prohibit a person convicted of animal welfare offenses from owning animals in the future. Other countries, such as England and Wales, have looked to New

Zealand in developing their own models of animal welfare legislation.

Ian trained originally as a veterinarian and managed a successful chain of veterinary clinics in New Zealand. His interest in educating the public in the care of animals led to a media career and his role as the "face of veterinary medicine" for almost ten years. He made regular appearances on television and radio programs, and published columns in newspapers and magazines on how to care for animals, veterinary medicine, and a host of other animal-related topics.

Ian's reach expanded internationally when a United States television network chose him to be one of a few television presenters introducing endangered species from around the world. His work on the program broadened his interest in animal issues, particularly in areas of the law. His interactions with scientists, politicians, and lawyers provided him with unique insights as to how the interests of many stakeholders, including animal-related businesses and animals themselves, were addressed (or not) by the law. He recognized the importance of animal welfare as a critical subject both nationally and internationally, and foresaw the growth of animal law in the shifting legal and social landscapes. At the time, there were no specific courses at schools in New Zealand, but with the goal of contributing to the development of the field, he decided to go to law school to gain whatever knowledge was available. So, in a major career move, he sold his veterinary clinics and became a law student.

Ian completed his law degree and in 2002 became an enrolled Barrister and Solicitor of the High Court of New Zealand. He has combined his legal and veterinary expertise, his business acumen, and his concern for animals to create a successful multi-faceted business and a reputation as an international animal law expert. Ian has remained true to his original purpose in becoming a lawyer and, in addition to his for-profit business, gives substantial time to advance the expansion and recognition of animal law as a legal specialty internationally.

Ian wrote and taught New Zealand's first course on animal law at the University of Canterbury in New Zealand. The course has since been taught at law and veterinary schools around the world. Ian continues to teach at the School of Law at the University of Leeds in England.

Ian is the founder and director of International Animal Law (IAL), a nonprofit organization working to improve animal welfare through a number of initiatives. IAL offers opportunities for international networking of animal welfare experts and on-site and online education in animal law, ethics, and science to assist professionals and organizations. Ian is also an external consultant to the World Organization for Animal Health (OIE) Collaboration Centre, a member of the International Advisory Board of Compassion in World Farming, and a prosecutor for New Zealand's Ministry of Agriculture and Forestry on cases involving matters of biosecurity and animal welfare.

Ian speaks regularly on a variety of animal law issues including enforcement and compliance, sustainable and humane animal welfare law, the role of the professional in contemporary issues such as the link between animal abuse and domestic violence, and the development of "good law" regarding issues of animal welfare in the context of wider global concerns. Ian also publishes frequently; many of his articles can be found on IAL's website.

"We can shape the future by applying vision ***and*** *real-world principles to the human-animal welfare connection."*

Many "non-traditional" students return to school to start a second career that fulfills a lifelong dream or to engage in work that is more meaningful for them or to society. Ian's decision to become a lawyer was obviously the right one. He thoroughly enjoys his work, considering it "more than just a job, but a way I can make a difference." His prediction that animal law would grow and be a catalyst for the protection of animals has proven correct. Countries continue to pass laws and negotiate treaties and agreements with animal welfare in mind. He continues to communicate an international message about successful and humane animal welfare practices and is giving back to the world through his volunteer work.

So what can we take from Ian's success? What makes a successful entrepreneur in animal law? First of all, what makes a successful entrepreneur? There are endless books that have been published on the subject and purport to have the perfect profile of the entrepreneurial type. Words like visionary, free thinker, dreamer, risk taker, high energy, creative, and confident come up consistently, and all are probably true to a certain extent.

In Ian's situation, there are several components of his success. First, he took a subject he knew, animal care, and expanded on it. He took his veterinary knowledge and added legal skills. When surveying your options, focus on what you know, then consider how to expand and capitalize on it. Coupled with Ian's veterinary training was expertise in managing a business. This expertise is critical not only in running a business, but in presenting viable solutions to clients and stakeholders. Furthermore, many good ideas and noble intentions fail due to lack of funding, so learning how to be profitable or secure funding is essential to success. Make sure you know the ins and outs of running a business or find a partner who does.

Additionally, be clear about what you want to achieve. Have an end point, an ultimate goal beyond making money, such as furthering the field of animal law. Everything else you do centers on that goal.

Timing can also be a critical element of success—one that we cannot control, but one that we can recognize. Ian listened, and continues to listen, to people with knowledge and experience he did not have and saw where it might lead. Go to the people whose knowledge and expertise differ from yours, whether in science, politics, or business, and work that into your long-term plan. Animal law is still evolving and will continue to grow in various areas—agriculture, wildlife, entertainment, conservation, and more. Think about how to capitalize on that growth.

Also, doing what you know and love provides the foundation upon which everything else can be built. It is evident in the stories of all of the lawyers who are featured in this book that they enjoy what they do. That enjoyment and dedication is a strong motivator. While it may be difficult at first to do what you love full-time, you can at least begin by making it a part of your practice and your life. Ian practices law, he writes, he speaks, and he educates on animal welfare. He has never strayed far from what he knows and enjoys, which is furthering animal welfare. While the means change, the end has not.

Nonprofit Law

Another niche area of practice is nonprofit law, generally considered a subset of business or corporate law. Most humane organizations and rescue groups are tax-exempt nonprofits under section 501(c)(3) of the Internal Revenue Code. And while small organizations can, and often do, file their own applications, there are many organizations that engage the services of lawyers, not only for the original filings but also for the ongoing state and federal reports that are required. Federal reporting laws have been strengthened and nonprofits risk losing their exemptions if they do not comply with the regulations. In addition to the submission of the original application, the lawyer's role is to keep the nonprofit apprised of any changes in the law regarding their nonprofit status or reporting; draft and submit the required reports; and advise the client on issues, such as political activities, that may jeopardize their exempt status. Many nonprofits are small and have few resources, but there are also many nonprofits that have the resources to employ lawyers, or will have as they grow.

There are law firms that include nonprofit work as one of their areas of expertise. The ABA has a Nonprofit Committee within its Business Law Section.

Personal Injury/Civil Litigation

Litigation is an essential area of the practice of animal law. Animal issues are litigated at every level, from a local suit for the wrongful death of a companion animal to a suit to compel the enforcement of a federal animal protection statute. Trends indicate that litigation is on the rise, and lawyers with skills in civil litigation and personal injury law have valuable knowledge and expertise.

Wills, Trusts, and Estate Planning

Estate planning that includes provisions for the care of an animal in the event of the owner's death or disability is a relatively new concept. Many animal owners and lawyers are still unaware that specific laws have been enacted that recognize the legal validity of a trust established for the care of an animal. Previously, an owner could set up an honorary trust, but this type of trust was voluntary and might run afoul of the rule against perpetuities or other estate laws. They fell far short of the pet trusts that are legal today. This is a major change—the law now, in essence, recognizes an animal as a beneficiary. And as we learned from the Leona Helmsley case, lawyers need to be very specific when drafting wills and trusts that direct monies to the care of animals. In addition, clients need advice on options that are available in the event that they are unable, either temporarily or permanently, to care for their animals. Will bequests and agreements with friends and family members can be established in advance of an emergency.

Estate planning also includes working with clients who wish to establish trusts and gifts to animal welfare and humane organizations, jobs found in a law firm setting or as a legal consultant or staff attorney for nonprofit organizations that create legacy programs for their more affluent donors.

Follow the Animals

For some animal lawyers, the first step to a career is to follow their passion for an animal or species. Then they look for a way to construct a law practice around the animals. It may seem an odd approach at first, but consider other areas of practice—a family lawyer may have first been interested in children, or an environmental lawyer may have started with a love of the ocean.

Companion Animals

In the United States, companion animals occupy a large part of the public's involvement with animals. When we think of a companion animal, it's usually a cat or a dog that comes to mind, but what we consider "companions" may include goldfish, hamsters, ferrets, and all kinds of exotic animals. Solo practitioners in animal law devote most of their time to companion animal cases. Clients may include individuals, rescue groups, breeders, veterinarians, and suppliers of goods and services, from pet food to pet sitting.

States and municipalities have been active in recent years in passing laws related to companion animals, and there appears to be no slowdown in the enactment of laws concerning commercial breeding, spaying/neutering, tethering, dangerous dogs, and breed-specific legislation. All of these issues will continue to occupy lawmakers and the public as debates continue about our property right in animals and our treatment of them.

Farm Animals

In some parts of the country farming dominates the landscape, economy, and mindset of those who live there. When we think of farming, many of us still imagine cows lazily grazing in green meadows. Unfortunately, the increasing demand for meat at a cheaper price has resulted in animal confinement and production methods that are considered cruel and inhumane by many advocates. The issue is a contentious and controversial one, as animal welfare organizations and the public, through voter initiatives, pressure the agriculture industry to institute more humane methods of treatment for farm animals. Laws, such as California's Proposition 2, have mandated better conditions for farm animals, but the agriculture industry challenges these efforts in the media and in the courts.

Consequently, a career in factory farming is not a "grey area" where animal protection law is concerned. Clear lines have been drawn between animal advocates, who overwhelmingly see factory farming as cruel, and the agriculture industry, which is fighting efforts to change its treatment of animals used for food. If you are interested in working with farm animals, carefully research the industry and understand the issues and controversies.

If you are focused on the protection of farm animals, there are humane organizations such as Farm Sanctuary, whose specific mission is to rescue and protect farm animals. The organization has two sanctuaries where farm animals live out their lives in a natural setting. If you are opposed to factory farming practices, but believe that animals may be used for food if treated humanely, one alternative to the factory farm environment is the sustainable farm. Animals are still raised for food, but their treatment varies drastically from the high-production confinement methods used in factory farms. Cows are allowed to openly graze on grass, their natural food, rather than fed corn in condensed housing environments. Chickens and pigs are allowed to roam and engage in behavior that is natural to them; that is, to act like chickens and pigs. The animals are not treated with antibiotics or hormones. The sustainable farm concept is a growing, but still relatively small industry. For the lawyer-entrepreneur who is interested in farm animals, this industry may be worth investigating. The Niman Ranch is one example of a sustainable farm that, according to its website, started small in the 1970s and now has 650 independent farmers and ranchers raising animals within the humane standards set by Niman. Also expanding are organic and natural grocers such as Whole Foods, which purchase meat from sustainable farms.

Horses

Equine law is an old established area of the law, perhaps the original animal law. In the past, an equine lawyer was a lawyer who negotiated contracts for the sale, care, and breeding of horses, and was based in the states where these activities largely took place, such as Kentucky. Today's equine lawyer does much more. Equine lawyers still deal with contracts, but they also deal with insurance issues, intellectual property, and tax implications. Lawyers also handle veterinary malpractice cases, which may involve significant amounts of money where horses are concerned.

Work to protect horses, whether in racing environments or roaming the wild plains, is more widespread today. Horse rescue has become urgent due to the number of horses being abandoned or starved by owners who can no longer take care of them. The slaughter of horses for human consumption is now illegal in the United States, but the debate continues as advocates and business interests argue that more horses are starving or being slaughtered inhumanely in Mexico and Canada. All of these issues require lawyers who know the law and know horses.

Ocean Life

What if you have a passion for whales? Are you concerned with overfishing? There are legal issues surrounding the harvesting of marine mammals and the near-extinction of several species of fish at the international, national, and even state levels. Certain whale species are still endangered, although there has been an international moratorium on commercial whaling since 1982.

Beyond conservation, there is an ongoing controversy among countries regarding how humans should treat sea mammals, such as whales and dolphins, based on scientific research regarding their advanced intelligence. Battles are being waged on the open seas between whaling countries and preservationists, who feel they have a moral duty to protect these creatures. Whale watching continues to grow in popularity worldwide, even in whaling countries, although some say to the whales' detriment. United States tourism experts say whale watching is a $2 billion tourist industry. Whales also continue to be top attractions at aquatic parks. The fight to save the whales involves cultural, ethical, and legal issues that will not be resolved any time soon.

Not attracted to whales? What about dolphins? Or tuna? Or salmon? All of these sea dwellers are the subjects of legal issues related to commercial fishing, conservation, and commerce. Overfishing is of major concern today to conservationists and fisheries alike. Many species of fish are near extinction; international cooperation is required to save them.

The following career profile tells the story of one lawyer whose passion for an ocean mammal led to a successful practice in animal law. His story is a lesson in following the animal, taking risks, building a law business, and finding success.

Career Profile

James F. Gesualdi, Attorney at Law
Islip, Long Island, New York

For Jim Gesualdi, a trip to the Florida Keys transformed his lifelong passion for dolphins into a successful career in animal law. His experiences on that trip in 1989 changed Jim's priorities. He spent a week in Florida working with cancer patients, who taught him what was important in life. Also on that trip, he witnessed first-hand the intelligence and grace of dolphins, sea mammals that showed him what was important in his career. He met "Little Bit," the last dolphin from the *Flipper* television show.

Jim was a large firm lawyer and had never thought of himself as an animal law practitioner, but his experiences in Florida motivated him to undertake substantial pro bono work in the field. He loved the animals and eventually chose to pursue a career in which he could work directly to promote enhanced animal welfare and conservation, especially for dolphins and other animals in zoological institutions and the wild. He focused on the practical aspects of making it happen by developing what he termed a "blueprint" for the practice he wanted. First, he determined the various areas of the law that he would use in a practice. He then listed his legal expertise, making note of those activities he enjoyed and those he did not. Once he decided on the areas of expertise that comprised his ideal animal law practice, he listed the people, resources, and opportunities to make it happen.

Second, he outlined what he would need to learn about animals and the relevant laws that protect them. As he got into it, he realized he had a great deal to learn. Once familiar with the laws governing marine mammals, he began to study them, along with the accompanying regulations. In his research, he found laws and regulations that posed challenges relating to implementation, administration, and enforcement. As a way to promote his knowledge and understanding of the complex statutory and regulatory issues, he wrote briefings presenting the problems he saw and setting out solutions. He then sent the briefings to organizations he thought would be interested.

Jim was correct. His writings, including informal treatises on the Animal Welfare Act and the Marine Mammal Protection Act regulations, were of great interest to his targeted organizations. And as can often happen in an emerging field such as animal law, Jim became an expert in these areas and participated in the landmark U.S. Department of Agriculture Marine Mammal Negotiated Rulemaking. He readily joined representatives from zoos, aquariums, trade organizations, the U.S. Navy, federal regulatory agencies, and other animal organizations in drafting revisions to the Marine Mammal Regulations under the Animal Welfare Act. The process gave him insight into the views of the participants and the government, as well as familiarity with the new regulations. This was a turning point in his career. Jim's direct involvement provided him with the valuable background necessary for subsequent analysis and commentary relevant to the new rules. He became an irreplaceable asset to the organizations that would have to comply with the rules.

Today, Jim is a sole practitioner with an animal law practice, once just a rough idea on his blueprint for the future of his practice. His knowledge, passion, volunteering, and networking efforts attracted clients and resulted in the satisfying career he envisioned. His practice involves very little litigation, which he generally refers to a colleague. His greatest emphasis is on administrative work involving regulatory and enforcement issues relating to animal welfare and conservation.

He starts his day in front of a computer, monitoring the news and events affecting his clients. Beyond the expected correspondence, telephone calls, and research, Jim devotes a significant amount of time to anticipating legal and other issues his clients and other stakeholders may face and developing creative solutions to those issues before they arise. Creative thinking is a foundation around which everything else revolves. For example, Jim often reviews proposed and new regulations to assess "real world" administration and implementation issues, as well as possible unintended consequences. Familiarity with all aspects of the regulatory process helps make such reviews more constructive.

Many animal advocates and lawyers have developed satisfying careers that were prompted by an experience or experiences that changed their thinking and life's direction profoundly. Jim's story is just one of many.

"There are limitless meaningful opportunities for making a difference for animals and people. Commitment, creativity, passion, persistence, and constructive professionalism are the keys."

Working for aquariums, zoos, and their related trade organizations involves an in-depth knowledge of the various regulatory issues affecting these organizations. Federal, state, and local laws, as well as international laws and treaties govern the transfer and care of animals in these settings. Some of the organizations are for-profit and some are nonprofit, furthering the complexity in providing legal services. Practitioners in this field counsel clients on laws, licensing, and permit issues; enforcement situations; import and export laws; conservation; and more. (Jim has also worked with a number of individuals and diverse organizations beyond zoological institutions because of his animal welfare experience.)

Work for these types of organizations can be done in a solo setting or within a firm; incomes will vary depending on the environment. Lawyers in this area are likely to spend a great deal of time in front of a computer or documents. They must stay abreast of changes in the law, review current litigation, and evaluate the actions and events that effect zoological institutions and the animals in their care, as well as those in the wild. Building a practice and successfully working in this area also involves a tremendous amount of relationship building with clients and others.

Jim sees working with these organizations as opportunities to promote animal welfare and conservation and facilitate change from the inside where possible. As with all entities involved with animals and animal law, there may also be opportunities to work on legal matters for the organization that may not relate directly to animals (e.g., contracts, labor issues).

The field is not saturated, but it is limited. There are finite numbers of zoos, aquariums, and trade organizations located in major metropolitan areas. In addition to aquariums and zoos, however, animals are used for entertainment in game parks, movies, television, and sports franchises.

Wild Animals

Do you watch every wild animal program on television? Is your dream vacation one of trudging through the muddy rainforests of Uganda to see the gorillas? Perhaps a career involving wild animals is for you. In addition to their lives in the wild, they are in found in sanctuaries, parks, zoos, and aquariums, as well as in circuses and other entertainment arenas. They still roam openly in some of the national and state parks and remaining wilderness areas in the United States. For the international job seeker, they are found in areas all over the world, including Asia, Africa, and Indonesia.

Following whatever passion you have for animals may lead you to the career you want. If you can volunteer, the experience will lead you to people who work with the animals you care about and help you determine whether or not it is the right fit for you.

Having a passion for a certain animal or animals has driven the careers of many researchers, scientists, and biologists. One thinks of Dian Fossey's work with gorillas and Jane Goodall's research on chimpanzees. Their passions resulted in life-long missions, furthered the causes of the animals they loved, brought new awareness to animal issues, and sparked the passions of others.

There is no reason why that same passion cannot fuel success in animal law.

The Law Firm

Going Solo

Setting up a solo law firm is exciting and challenging, regardless of the type of law you plan to practice. If you just graduated from law school and passed the bar you have the educational and professional credentials, but lack hands-on legal experience and usually the financial resources to sustain you until you develop your practice. You may also have student loans to be repaid and other obligations that will not wait. Therefore, it may be advisable to spend a few years at a law firm, a government job, or other legal job gaining an education, making contacts, and building experience before launching a solo practice in animal law.

However, if you decide to take the plunge, or you are not a new lawyer and have the experience, resources, and drive to go solo, do your homework. Talk with other lawyers and read the advice of the experts. The ABA and your local bar groups have books and educational programs on everything from avoiding malpractice to finding business via the Internet. The more you know, the more likely you are to succeed, and there is no reason not to learn from others' mistakes as opposed to making them yourself.

While some cases, such pet trusts and contract matters, may not involve litigation, most animal cases do involve trial work. The solo practitioner with an animal law practice should enjoy litigation; otherwise, consider another career option. Much of the work of the solo practitioner involves litigation; it will be difficult to narrow your focus to non-litigation cases unless you expand beyond animal law.

If you decide to start an animal law practice for companion animals, you can expect to handle some or all of the following types of cases:

- Veterinary malpractice for injury or death of a companion animal;
- Wrongful death or injury involving breeders, animal boarding facilities, groomers, retailers, and manufacturers;

- Consumer fraud or products liability involving breeders and manufacturers of products such as toys, food, or other products and services;
- Defense of animal rights protestors;
- Ownership and custody disputes;
- Landlord/tenant and homeowner association issues;
- Local ordinance violations such as dangerous dog hearings and nuisance cases;
- Contract evaluation, negotiation, and other issues for rescue groups and other nonprofits; and
- Pet trusts and emergency planning.

Part of your financial success will depend on the city and state where you establish your practice. State laws and legal precedent regarding veterinary malpractice, damages for companion animals, and the award of attorneys' fees vary by state and will affect your income. Also, both the size and prosperity of the city in which you practice and how the city's residents feel about the value of their companion animals will affect your business. Know your city's "animal welfare" culture. What kind of animal shelter does it have? How often are animal issues covered in the media? Does the local bar have an animal law section? What is the city's record in animal cruelty prosecutions? Are there other animal law practitioners? What animal welfare nonprofits are based there? Before starting a practice, research the legal situation and market environment to gain the knowledge to handle the cases *and* to evaluate your income potential, and read the following profile.

Career Profile

Adam Karp, Principal
The Animal Law Offices of Adam Karp
Bellingham, Washington

The hazards of starting a new law firm notwithstanding, Adam Karp opened the Animal Law Offices of Adam Karp in 2000 after obtaining a master's degree in statistics following law school. He developed an interest in animal welfare while in graduate school and knew he wanted to start an animal law practice when he graduated. He never considered another option.

For Adam, animal law is animal protection law. While agreeing with the standard definition of animal law, he sees more. He further distinguishes animal law as a method of practice, how a lawyer approaches the case—ethically, procedurally, and substantively. Some animal law, such as that practiced in agriculture, is approached from an animal use perspective. Adam approaches his cases—and decides whether he accepts them and how he handles them—from an animal welfare perspective. While animal law encompasses a variety of perspectives, the lawyer's methods and approaches are the distinctions that separate those who practice.

When Adam started to promote his firm he knew that community education and publicity would be two major components. While animal law was new, the public's interest and the media's coverage of animal issues were not new. He offered his expertise to the media and they responded. Adam became the "go-to" lawyer for animal stories and he continues to appear regularly on television and is often quoted in newspaper reports.

When starting a law practice, particularly in a new field such as animal law, it is important to understand the value of the media and how it works. While paid advertising can generate business, free media publicity, such as giving advice and expert opinions in newspaper articles and television news stories, carries additional credibility not found in advertising. Working with the media involves providing reporters with what they want when they need it, which is learned in part through reading their columns and watching their coverage of the issues. By responding promptly to their requests and providing them with valuable and accurate information, you will become the "expert" they turn to for animal issues. Soon, your name becomes familiar to the public and to potential clients.

In addition to looking at how he could advance his personal career, Adam also looked at what he could do in his community to further animal welfare and promote the field of animal law. He started an animal law section in the state of Washington, raising awareness among the state's lawyers. Even today, many lawyers are still not knowledgeable about the practice of animal law. Bringing lawyers together with like interests and educating them helped highlight his practice and generate referrals. He developed a website and placed telephone listings in directories under the heading "Animal Law." Adam also took pro bono cases, wrote articles, and volunteered with animal law professional organizations. His efforts paid off, and today he has a successful solo practice and also contributes to the national development of animal law.

Adam's successful practice answers the question many lawyers ask regarding animal law: "Can you make a living?" Adam has been practicing animal law for ten years, proof that it can be done. His fees are based on contingency, hourly rates, and set fee agreements, and he still handles some pro bono cases.

Starting a practice in 2000 made Adam one of the early pioneers in animal law. He continues to manage his business and his clients single handedly. There is no typical day for Adam except a full one. In addition to a regular caseload of 20–30 clients, he receives anywhere from three to ten calls and/or emails each week regarding legal representation. He evaluates and accepts cases based on his animal welfare standards and concerns. He continues to offer advice and support to the field through his involvement with the ABA TIPS Animal Law Committee, where he is vice-chair. He co-authors "Recent Developments in Animal Tort and Insurance Law" published in the ABA *Tort, Trial & Insurance Practice Law Journal* every year. And in his spare time, he supports his local animal welfare organizations.

Adam advises new lawyers to consider spending a few years litigating and learning the many relevant areas of the law before starting a practice. Given the broad legal reach of animal law and the lack of more than basic survey courses in law school, it is important for new lawyers to spend time honing their legal skills. Find other lawyers with experience in animal law. It remains a small community of lawyers, all of whom are more than happy to share their expertise. Write articles and study an area that will help position you as an expert. Animal law remains one of the few areas of the law in which that is possible.

In handling cases, a high level of self-esteem is an important characteristic. More cases are lost in animal law than in other areas of practice due in part to the legal status of animals as property and legal barriers to standing. The lawyer must be able to mentally leave the case and move on to the next one. Also, the advice to "know your client" takes on a special meaning. Most lawyers deal with one species—humans. Animal lawyers may have several—dogs, cats, horses, pigs, or even elephants—in addition to the human client. So in animal law, "know your client" means taking the time to educate yourself about the human client *and* the animal—the behavior, biology, and physiology of the focus of your case.

"Fiat justicia ruat caelum." (May justice be done though the heavens fall.)

Find a Partner

While Adam chose the solo practice route, another option to consider is starting a firm with another lawyer or group of lawyers. Perhaps one of the lawyers at your firm or a classmate from law school shares your interest in animal law and/or starting a firm.

A group of lawyers can combine their talents to create a dynamic and unique law firm specializing in animal law plus other areas of practice. Sharing the expenses and dividing the legal responsibilities is much easier and can be more effective with two or more lawyers than going it alone.

In the Firm

After reading about Adam's solo practice, starting a firm in animal law may not be practical or economically feasible for you. Unless you have clients on board, starting a law firm requires financial resources for start-up costs and to sustain you until paying clients are on the books. Marketing skills are a must. Animal law requires an even greater promotional and educational effort because the field is still new. It requires networking and educating other lawyers so they will refer business to you, and educating the public so that they know what animal law is and that you are open for business. All of these activities take time, in addition to handling clients. It is also a field that may require some pro bono or reduced-fee work to get established.

However, if you are at a law firm, you may be able to ease into an animal law practice by adding clients to your existing caseload. For the civil litigator, there are many relevant cases such as dangerous dog hearings, consumer fraud, contract disputes, and veterinary malpractice that will fit easily within the litigator's area of practice. For transactional lawyers, drafting contracts, advising nonprofits on various issues, or becoming involved in legislative issues are ways to expand a practice and enhance your expertise in animal law. Transactional lawyers can also advise clients on landlord/tenant issues and homeowner association rules.

The following profile shows how one lawyer started the day as a "meat-eating, milkshake-loving barbequer with leather boots" and ended the day as a "soy-eating, vegan animal lawyer with a mission."

Career Profile

Bruce Wagman, Partner
Schiff Hardin LLP
San Francisco, California

Bruce Wagman is an established animal protection lawyer. He has grown up with animal law, contributed to its development, and practices it almost exclusively as a partner in the San Francisco office of Schiff Hardin LLP, a national 400-lawyer firm based in Chicago.

After starting a career as an operating room nurse, Bruce soon realized that he was not suited for the medical field. He began to think of possible jobs that would provide the financial support he needed along with the intellectual challenges he wanted in a career. He decided to become a lawyer and graduated from Hastings Law School in 1991.

While in law school, Bruce became interested in practicing in a social justice field, but had not yet decided on a specific direction. After graduating, he accepted a clerkship with federal district court judge William H. Orrick of the Northern District of California to gain experience and contemplate his next move. It was during his clerkship that his future came to him in what he calls a "revelation." In 1992, out of curiosity, he attended a session on "Animal Rights Law" at an ABA conference. The speakers described the ongoing institutional cruelty that was being committed against animals in farming and commercial breeding, as well as by individuals—and very little was being done. He considered himself an animal lover and was struck by his lack of awareness of the tragic plight of many animals. He left the session a different person, determined to use his legal career to challenge the injustices that were being inflicted on animals.

The evolution of Bruce's career spans a time of significant transformation in the field. The law, the lawyers, and the stakeholders have grown and changed considerably over the last twenty years. In 1992, when Bruce began his practice, animal law cases were handled typically on a part-time, pro bono basis by a few lawyers scattered throughout the country. The Animal Legal Defense Fund, a nonprofit organization dedicated to fighting animal cruelty through the legal system, had been around since the late 1970s, but had only recently started to gain momentum and wide exposure. It was still a very new area of practice, but had begun to spark some interest in the legal community. For example, the ABA had sponsored the educational session on animal rights law that inspired Bruce, and Lewis & Clark College of Law in Portland, Oregon, held its first animal law conference in 1995. But that was unusual; only a few law schools offered classes, and there was no casebook. Most local and state bar associations had yet to establish animal law sections or committees. Books, journals, and law review articles on animals and the law were in short supply. Finding relevant case law was also problematic because few opinions existed and those that were available often included facts that were not on point with current actions and laws. That was the state of animal law in 1992.

After completing his clerkship, Bruce joined the firm of Morgenstein & Jubelirer, a thirty-lawyer civil litigation firm in San Francisco, to learn civil litigation practice. Undeterred by the dearth of scholarship, legal precedent, resources, and fellow colleagues in the field, Bruce launched his animal law practice by writing every organization he could find that had the word "animal" in its name. He received a few affirmative responses for pro bono work, among them the Animal Legal Defense Fund. With animal law cases in tow and his first solid client, Bruce launched his law career.

Bruce started work with firm clients in the products liability and employment areas and pro bono cases in animal law. His early animal law work included a variety of cases related to companion animals. He found animal law to be incredibly complex and demanding. In addition to needing to know the basics of many areas of the law, bringing a living animal into the picture brought up new ethical, scientific, and philosophical issues and transformed the cases. His science background and medical experience helped him build his practice as he took on the task of learning the physiology and psychology of cats, dogs, dolphins, chimpanzees, and elephants. He also had to deal with what he terms a "schizophrenia in the law," where a species of animal may be treated one way in one state and another way in another state; or how it is legally acceptable to treat a farm animal in a certain manner, but that same treatment of a companion animal would be egregious and illegal animal cruelty. These complexities and challenges, along with the satisfaction of helping animals, energized and motivated him to devote virtually all of his time to animal cases.

After a few years, word spread of Bruce's unique area of expertise and he developed a successful animal law practice. His knowledge and hard work, combined with the public's increasing interest in animal protection, attracted paying clients. Major animal welfare organizations retained him to represent them in litigation, contract, and other matters. He also became involved in legislative work, which is today a significant component of the animal welfare agenda at local, state, and federal levels.

While his practice grew, the field of animal law grew as well. Bruce's expertise was in demand and he began to freely share his knowledge with animal lawyers and welfare groups around the country. In 1996 he began teaching animal law at Hastings College of Law, where the class has been offered every fall semester for the last fifteen years. He has taught at four Bay Area law schools and now alternates among three. In 2000, he co-authored the first animal law casebook, *Animal Law: Cases and Materials*, which is now in its fourth edition. His most recent work is *A World View of Animal Law*, co-authored with Matthew Liebman. The book is a survey of the way different countries and cultures treat animals under the law. He is one of the most experienced and knowledgeable lawyers in the field. In addition to his routine work, he devotes much of his time consulting with humane organizations and speaking at conferences and events around the country.

Bruce's primary work is that of a civil litigator. His days are spent like any other litigator, except that his cases involve animals. The issues are complex, making them intellectually and legally challenging. His advice to law students or new lawyers who want to practice animal law is to take it seriously and hone your legal skills first, then your animal law skills. A lack of knowledge about a specific ordinance or law can result in the death of an animal or bad legal precedent. Animal law is still evolving, and even the most insignificant case can turn up in a U.S. Supreme Court brief for lack of any other precedent available to the court.

An animal law practitioner must be particularly thick skinned. Horrific instances of animal cruelty; the killing, abandonment, and neglect of healthy dogs and cats; and indifference on the part of the public are all facts of life for the animal lawyer and come with an emotional toll. Cases are lost due to lack of standing, the political or financial power of the opposition, or irrational public fears. You must have a big picture view of the work and the ability to celebrate when you win and move on when you don't.

Bruce's start in animal law coincided with the start of tremendous growth and interest in the field. He was in California, a state where the animal welfare movement had momentum. There was a tremendous opportunity to teach, to contribute to the case law and scholarship, and to mount significant legal challenges against the cultural and societal mistreatment of animals. Opportunities still exist, but they are different. While still evolving, most animal lawyers believe that animal law and the animal welfare movement have matured and that animal law is entering a new stage in its evolution.

In looking ahead, Bruce sees greater legal scholarship—discourse that stimulates our thinking, raises questions, and presents new ideas—as one of the key needs for animal law's future advancement. Illustrating animal law's fascinating and challenging legal issues will lead to greater exposure and acceptance by law firms, academics, and law students. Animal law incorporates the legal philosophies of the civil rights and environmental movements, and greater scholarship will highlight its unique character.

"Working for animals is less about working and more about following a passion. That makes it a calling, not just a profession."

Working for a Nonprofit Humane Organization

According to the National Center for Charitable Statistics, there are 18,553 animal-related charities in the United States. There are more than 100 listed in Appendix C of this book. Local rescue groups, animal welfare organizations, and sanctuaries exist throughout the country working to place or shelter abandoned dogs, cats, birds, and exotic wildlife such as tigers and chimpanzees. Some of the organizations have paid staff attorneys and in-house counsel, but the smaller ones rely on pro bono work or use their best judgment when situations arise. The following profiles highlight six humane organizations, presented to illustrate varying types of organizations and how they differ in history, mission, and goals.

The American Society for the Prevention of Cruelty to Animals

The American Society for the Prevention of Cruelty to Animals (ASPCA) was established in 1866 and was the first humane organization in North America. It claims a number of *firsts*, including being the first organization to be granted legal authority to investigate and make arrests for crimes against animals. The ASPCA's stated mission from the nineteenth to the twenty-first century has been to "provide effective means for the prevention of cruelty to animals" and to fulfill that mission through nonviolent means. The organization's programs are centered on three areas: (1) caring for pet parents and pets, (2) providing positive outcomes for at-risk animals, and (3) serving victims of animal cruelty.

The APSCA has a number of staff attorneys that serve in different capacities. Headquartered in New York City, the organization has two lawyers who serve as in-house counsel. In addition, a trusts and estates lawyer handles the organization's bequests and trusts from donors. The Humane Law Enforcement Division is focused on animal cruelty prosecutions in New York City and employs two criminal law lawyers. These lawyers advise humane law enforcement agents on proper criminal procedure and constitutional directives and assist prosecutors in prosecuting cases. The Government Relations Department is divided by region and employs four lawyers who monitor legislative activities at the state and federal levels, draft new legislation, and lobby for its passage.

Animal Legal Defense Fund

The Animal Legal Defense Fund (ALDF) is a nonprofit organization that has been "fighting to protect the lives and advance the interests of animals through the legal system" for more than three decades. ALDF is based in the San Francisco Bay Area and also has an office in Portland, Oregon. Their primary programs are the Litigation Program, Criminal Justice Program, and Animal Law Program. ALDF lawyers file lawsuits to "stop the abuse of companion animals, and animals abused in industries including factory farming and the entertainment business." They also provide free legal assistance to prosecutors handling cruelty cases and work to strengthen state anti-cruelty statutes. Their law student program to nurture the future of animal law, the Student Animal Legal Defense Fund, is covered in Chapter 4.

Career Profile

Joyce Tischler, Founder, General Counsel
Animal Legal Defense Fund
Cotati, California

Few people can say they started a movement. Joyce Tischler, along with a small group of lawyers, not only started a movement, but launched a legal discipline—animal law. It has grown into a field of law that is recognized both nationally and internationally. The lawyers who formed what is now the Animal Legal Defense Fund (ALDF) combined their concern for animals with their legal training to use the courts to aggressively pursue greater protection for animals. They were so successful that using the legal system to fight for animals is now routine. At the time, however, nothing about it was routine. Everything was so new that these lawyers first had to educate themselves on the relevant law in order to litigate the cases.

That was thirty years ago, but Joyce's history of caring for animals began long before ALDF. She has had a lifelong involvement with animals, dating back to her childhood. Always volunteering, she helped run a shelter for cats while in college. In law school she wrote a law review article on a guardianship model for dogs and cats, a subject far ahead of its time.

For Joyce, Peter Singer's book, *Animal Liberation*, was inspirational. First published in 1975 and now in its third printing, Singer brought to light as no one else had the cruelty that was being inflicted on animals used for food and in scientific research. The book revealed that the laws designed to protect animals from cruelty, such as the Animal Welfare Act, were being ignored by those inflicting the cruelty and those charged with preventing it. Singer's message resonated with many advocates and proved to be prophetic for Joyce.

Upon graduating from law school, she joined an Oakland law firm as an associate and continued her volunteer work with Fund for Animals. It was there that she met Larry Kessenick, another lawyer interested in animal rights. That prompted an effort to find other lawyers. They sent out a notice to see if other lawyers were interested in animal rights, and soon a group of eight animal rights lawyers convened to change the plight of animals.[2]

Since that time Joyce has had years of experience fighting animal cruelty in the courts at the local, state, and federal levels. When asked about changes over the years in animal-related litigation, she sees a strategy that has evolved in some ways and in some ways has not. The most recent tactic is to litigate the more narrowly targeted, and winnable, cases. But she still sees a need to litigate the big cases. While they may be lost for lack of standing or on the merits, she believes that it is important to continue to "push the envelope" and build a foundation for future litigation. Also, in the area of private practice, animal-related litigation on behalf of individuals is now well established. Lawyers are filing innovative suits to serve their clients and to push for new precedent and changes in the law.

Animal law is also evolving into a field that is more focused and specialized. In the beginning there was so much work to be done by so few lawyers that animal

---

[2] *See* Joyce Tischler, *The History of Animal Law Part 1: 1972–1987*, Volume 1 Stanford J. Animal L. & Pol'y 1 (2008).

law was everything to everyone. Today the trend is to specialize—by animals, such as companion animals or farm animals, or by law, such as criminal prosecution. This trend is important because it gives animal lawyers the level of expertise needed to be more effective as they go up against lawyers who specialize.

Joyce has worn many hats with ALDF over the years. She holds the title of general counsel and continues to serve as an advisor on litigation issues. Her current role, and where she feels she can be most productive, is in seeking out new opportunities for ALDF. Animal law and animal protection issues are now international in scope, and she talks with lawyers all over the world. One particularly exciting project is a series of symposia on animals used in scientific research. In 2007, the National Research Council issued a report on toxicity testing. The report found that revolutions in biology and biotechnology could eliminate or largely reduce toxicity testing on animals due to the superiority of using in vitro methods instead. The ALDF, Center for Animal Law Studies at Lewis & Clark Law School, Johns Hopkins University Center for Alternatives to Animal Testing, and Environmental Law Institute are collaborating on symposia and publications in an effort to create momentum for this change in animal testing. Litigation in this area has been disappointing and this project holds much promise.

ALDF is stronger than ever. With six staff attorneys handling everything from litigation to pro bono recruitment to education, the organization is well positioned for the future. While possessive of the organization she has nurtured and built, when asked if there is room for another one, she said honestly, "the more the merrier." She sees enormous opportunities for growth at the state level. Currently the bar organizations are filling the role, but progress is limited given that it is an after-hours commitment.

In addition to her work with ALDF, Joyce has turned her attention to big-picture issues, taking time she never had to think and write. She is working on part two of the history of animal law and will be working on a book and other writing projects in 2011. A combination of talent, determination, and a little luck has given Joyce a career that many of us hope for. Her advice to law students and others who want to work in animal law? Be creative. Those who want it will make it happen. And this author would add to that, "learn from Joyce."

I am sometimes asked: "If you care about others, why don't you focus on human suffering first"? My answer is that I am working at the roots. I work for animals precisely because most people choose to ignore their suffering.

Farm Sanctuary

Efforts to protect farm animals from cruel and inhumane treatment have gained momentum in recent years. The work of animal advocates has resulted in the passage of state laws and voter initiatives that have led to gradual improvements in conditions and significant advances in awareness of the treatment of farm animals.

One of the organizations that has worked for humane treatment of farm animals is Farm Sanctuary, which was established in 1986. The organization works to protect farm animals from cruelty, inspire change in the way society views and treats farm animals, and promote compassionate vegan living. Farm Sanctuary has several programs: a campaign to ban the marketing and slaughter of downed cattle (cows unable to stand on their own due to illness, injury, or other reason); two sanctuaries, in New York and California; a home adoption and placement program; and legislative campaigns to address issues such as anti-confinement, truth behind food labeling, and green foods.

Farm Sanctuary has one staff attorney who does advocacy work. They hire outside lawyers for specific projects and occasionally work with pro bono lawyers.

The Humane Society of the United States

For students and lawyers hoping to work for a nonprofit humane organization, a job at the Humane Society of the United States (HSUS) may be one of the most coveted. Established in 1954, HSUS is supported by 11 million Americans and is the largest animal protection organization in the United States. HSUS works to reduce animal suffering and create "meaningful social change for animals." They accomplish their goals by "advocating for sensible public policies, investigating cruelty and working to enforce existing laws, educating the public about animal issues, joining with corporations on behalf of animal-friendly policies, and conducting hands-on programs that make ours a more humane world."

While the organization has been in existence for more than fifty years, it was not until 2005 that the HSUS litigation team was formed to support its mission to fight animal abuse in state and federal courts throughout the country. Five years later, a team of three lawyers has grown to twenty-five, with Jonathan Lovvorn, HSUS vice president and chief counsel, leading the team's efforts.

Career Profile

Jonathan R. Lovvorn, Vice President and Chief Counsel
The Humane Society of the United States
Washington, D.C.

If working as a staff attorney for the Humane Society is a coveted job, then Jonathan Lovvorn's job as chief counsel must be the most coveted. However, Jonathan is quick to divert any attention away from himself and direct it to his staff attorneys and the many lawyers around the country who volunteer their time and resources to support the legal activities of HSUS.

Jonathan began his legal career in environmental law, and that is the lens through which he sees animal law. He takes a broad view of animal law as "any interaction between animals and the legal system" and adds "without a moral or policy position." When he was in law school, animal law was not a recognized area of the law and students who were interested in animal welfare issues studied environmental law. After graduating from law school, he earned an LLM in Environmental Law and Policy and worked in environmental law until 2005. That year he was recruited by the Humane Society to head their new litigation division along with three staff attorneys.

Jonathan and the rest of the HSUS lawyers stay busy. At any given time, Jonathan and the HSUS litigation team will have as many as fifty cases on the docket. Humane Society lawyers are never bored, and a "day in the life" could be anything at any given time. Cases may include emergency lawsuits filed to protect animals in immediate danger, or long-term and focused campaigns to develop case law or defend legislation. Jonathan's work also requires some legislative analysis and reviewing legal advice provided by outside counsel. All of the cases and activities of the legal department closely track and support the overall goals and objectives of HSUS.

Lawyers with the Humane Society must be thick-skinned, determined, and driven. They must be able to deal quickly and effectively with setbacks. In animal protection law, the cases can be extremely difficult and the wins far apart. Nevertheless, and perhaps as an indication of their exceptional skill and perseverance, Jonathan and his team have won more than 80 percent of the more than fifty cases they have filed over the past five years. Most lawyers in the public interest sector see wins in one out of three, or even five cases.

Jonathan credits the success of the Humane Society's legal program to a "tool kit" and strategy appropriated from his environmental law days. There is a place and purpose for the big lawsuits that, if won, would result in massive shifts in the legal landscape for animals. However, judges are often reluctant to oblige such sweeping changes, and losses in big lawsuits can result in major setbacks. So from the beginning, the Humane Society's legal strategy has been to pick the big battles carefully and focus on "asking for a little" in order to make definitive progress where judges are willing to grant it. As a result, most of their big cases are commercial in nature—class actions—where small, individual cases can be aggregated and litigated under class action rules.

With twenty-five lawyers, the HSUS legal team is the largest legal team in the history of the animal protection movement. And given the national scope of the Humane Society's work, the organization uses a network of outside lawyers, retained and pro bono, who provide valuable legal services as an extension of their core team. According to Jonathan, the organization could not have achieved its successes so far without the support of their national network of pro bono lawyers.

The staff attorneys who work for the Humane Society have primarily come to the organization through internships and pro bono work. Jonathan generally takes six to eight law clerks in the summer and also provides placements for students whose law schools allow them to work full-time for academic credit in the spring and fall. Finally, the animal law program at Georgetown University Law Center, where Jonathan teaches, has a clinical component that allows students to get hands-on experience working on animal law cases. Depending on enrollment, the clinic may involve anywhere from seven to twelve students. All of these programs allow Jonathan and fellow staffers to evaluate potential hires.

True to his past, Jonathan finds that students with experience in environmental and animal law have an ideal set of skills. Animal law is still a new area of the law, and most law schools that do provide an exposure offer only survey courses. Students interested in practicing animal law should also consider taking courses in environmental law, as they provide valuable education in administrative law, federal actions, and public attitudes toward "non-human" causes.

For law students who want careers in animal welfare, Jonathan has three key pieces of advice. First, you must be able to control your debt to work in any public interest field. He sees debt as the biggest obstacle for students. Second, do not concentrate only on animal law as your first job. There are many areas of the law that can provide valuable experience and can be a stepping-stone to a career in animal law. And third, do not discount the criminal law path. The trial and litigation experience is priceless. Local and state prosecutors are creating special animal cruelty divisions and making a tremendous difference in the lives of animals through the prosecution of animal cruelty, dog fighting, and cockfighting.

Looking ahead, Jonathan is optimistic about animal law's future successes in the courts. He believes the animal protection lawyers of tomorrow will have to be even more skilled in the different aspects of the law. Consistent with the thoughts and comments of other animal lawyers in this book, Jonathan sees animal law as a field that is maturing and heading toward an increasingly legislative framework. This means there will still be litigation, but constitutional issues will ultimately take center stage. Jonathan's prediction is already being realized, as the passage of various state laws requiring greater protection for farm animals has resulted in litigation.

The Physicians Committee for Responsible Medicine

The Physicians Committee for Responsible Medicine (PCRM) consists of a group of doctors and laypersons working toward "compassionate and effective medical practice, research, and health promotion." Founded in 1975, PCRM encourages higher standards for ethics and effectiveness in research, opposes unethical human experiments, and promotes alternatives to animal research and animal testing. The organization has worked to stop gruesome animal experiments and promote non-animal methods in medical education. Currently, more than three-quarters of all U.S. medical schools have dropped their animal labs. PCRM also promotes preventive medicine and has led the way for reforms in federal nutrition policies.

PCRM's legal department serves two separate functions and employs three lawyers. First, PCRM files advocacy lawsuits, petitions federal agencies, and takes other legal actions to advance its missions of promoting a vegan diet and ending the use of animals in research and education. The department's other function is to serve as in-house counsel for PCRM and its related entities. The legal department ensures that PCRM and its affiliates comply with all obligations applicable to 501(c)(3) charities; attends to legal matters such as personnel issues, lobbying, estates, and contracts; and handles other legal issues that arise in the course of PCRM's business.

The World Society for the Protection of Animals

On the international front, the mission of the World Society for the Protection of Animals (WSPA) is to build a global welfare movement, which it has been promoting for more than thirty years. Its work is concentrated in regions of the world where few measures exist for animal protection. The work of WSPA is focused in four areas: (1) responsible pet ownership, humane stray management, and anti-cruelty; (2) commercial exploitation of wildlife; (3) farm animals, specifically intensive farming and slaughter; and (4) disaster management.

The organization is the world's largest alliance of animal welfare societies with seventeen offices and more than 1,000 member organizations in more than 150 countries. It has served as consultant to the United Nations and the Council of Europe; campaigned politically to convince governments to change their practices to promote animal welfare; helped people in international communities set up animal welfare groups; implemented education campaigns to facilitate positive changes in attitudes toward animals; and provided direct help to animals all over the world that have been abandoned or neglected in disasters.

A Final Note

Keep in mind that most nonprofits, even the larger ones, are very conscious of how they spend their money. This is due in part to their nonprofit status, which requires them to focus their donations on their charitable endeavors as opposed to administrative expenses. Lawyers who choose to go into public interest law do so not for the money, but for the contribution they make to society by helping those most vulnerable. These nonprofits usually depend on pro bono lawyers as well as in-house staff attorneys to handle their many cases. However, the rewards come not in money, but in other ways. While the salaries for these lawyers are low compared to most law firm and corporate jobs, studies show the "happiness and satisfaction" factor is high.

Working for the Government

There are many opportunities to work in animal-related fields for governments at the local, state, and federal levels. As you will see, these jobs often provide excellent hands-on training and experience in animal welfare and the law.

United States Federal Government

There are diverse legal and nonlegal positions related to animals within the federal government. There are careers for lawyers who want to work as lawyers, as well as careers for lawyers in nonlegal or non-practice positions where a legal education and experience are valuable assets and sometimes required for the job.

Jobs exist in the executive, judicial, and legislative branches of government, although the executive branch has the greatest potential. There are many sources of information, but one place to start in order to learn basic information about the government and its various departments is their main website, at **www.usa.gov**. You can explore various topics, look for services, link to job searches, and more.

The federal judicial branch includes the United States Supreme Court, lower courts, special courts, and their support organizations, which consist of the Administrative Office of the United States Courts, the Federal Judicial Center, and the U.S. Sentencing Commission. While there are many lawyers working in the judicial branch, animal-specific jobs are lacking.

The legislative branch includes the U.S. Senate, U.S. House of Representatives, and those agencies that support Congress. There are internships for students interested in politics, such as those available with the Senate Committee on Agriculture, Nutrition, and Forestry. In addition to the committees, there are various subcommittees that deal with farming and related issues.

The executive branch's departments and agencies offer the most opportunities to work in animal-related fields. Simply think of the fact that there are approximately 100 federal animal protection statutes that must be administered and it is easy to see how and why animal-related jobs exist, and why they are spread across various agencies and locations. Moreover, the work of the government grows as new laws are enacted and revisions are made to existing ones.

One of the obvious legal careers with the government is that of a litigator. The country is continually involved in civil litigation as either plaintiff or defendant in many animal issue cases. On the criminal side, several departments are involved in prosecutions of people who violate federal criminal laws, from dog fighting to international trade laws.

For lawyers who are not litigators there are other possibilities. The government purchases services and goods requiring the work of lawyers in drafting, reviewing, and negotiating agreements. Lawyers are also required to review and evaluate legislation. While some jobs may be somewhat removed from animal law, certain departments deal specifically with animal issues.

There are policy advisors and analysts throughout the government whose jobs are to advise legislators, agency secretaries, and senior officers on policy issues. While policy advisors do not practice law in the traditional sense, many of these positions require expertise and credentials in law, policy, and science, in addition to other qualifications unique to the job. In general, responsibilities of these advisors and analysts may include providing guidance on policy issues surrounding existing programs and laws; assisting in the development and implementation of new policies; engaging in research and analysis to support the decision-making process; and generating issue papers. A preliminary job search turns up legal-related jobs as attorney-advisors, contracting officers, and program analysts in a variety of departments, many in departments and agencies likely to include animal issues.

For an idea of the scope of animal protection and conservation jobs within the government, consider the evolution of a law. Every law starts with someone—a citizen, government employee, or legislator—who decides there is a need for a law. Once that idea is presented, administrators, lawyers, policy advisors, and other experts research and assess the law's potential policy, human resources, economic, political, and legal implications. If the analysis is favorable, then the bill has to be drafted, edited, and evaluated; then it is introduced, and debates and negotiations begin. If the sponsor garners the needed support of legislators, the president, and the public, it is passed and signed into law. Once the bill becomes law, advisors, lawyers, and a new round of experts and agencies promulgate rules, gather and evaluate public opinion, and publish the rules. The next step is to establish administrative, investigative, and enforcement procedures; negotiate contracts; and put the law into action. Once in place, it has to be administered. When violations are suspected, investigations are initiated and those that uncover violations are then referred to the U.S. Department of Justice or other departments for civil and criminal legal actions. Much of the work just described requires the expertise of lawyers in a variety of fields.

In addition to the internal work involved in making law, consider the work undertaken outside the federal government when a new bill is introduced. For an animal-related bill, lobbyists, affected corporations, humane organizations, contractors, universities, scientific research facilities, and state and local governments swing into action. These groups work to determine whether the law would be beneficial or harmful and what action, if any, should be taken. Many of these activities require the services of in-house counsel or outside lawyers to assess the potential law's impact, advise clients, and work to fight or support the bill.

Beyond the work surrounding the creation and enforcement of laws that have a direct impact on animal welfare, there are the laws that are enacted for other purposes, but have secondary consequences for animals. Consider the Americans with Disabilities Act and the Fair Housing Act. Provisions of these laws come into play when citizens with service animals are denied housing or appropriate work accommodations. Lawyers with expertise in specific areas such as housing or employment are needed to resolve these issues. Also, environmental laws can have direct or indirect consequences for animals through habitat destruction or conservation. All of these laws go through the same administrative and enforcement processes described for animal protection laws.

How to Search

The United States Bureau of Labor Statistics, at **www.bls.gov**, reports that the federal government has about two million civilian employees, excluding the U.S. Postal Service, and is the nation's largest employer. Entire books have been written devoted exclusively to helping people find government jobs. Therefore, it would be unrealistic to attempt to list every legal and nonlegal position doing animal-related work within every government department or agency. The following information provides an overview of the various departments and agencies that are most likely to involve primary or secondary work on animal-related issues. The goal is to highlight some of the possibilities, point you in the right direction, and help you generate creative career ideas in animal law.

The main resource for jobs is **www.USAJOBS.com**, the official job site of the U.S. federal government. In order to fully access the site, users must set up an account with a password and provide some personal information, such as name, address, and telephone number. Job seekers may simply browse a listing of available jobs or search by keyword and/or location without registering. Some of the animal-related jobs require a science or research background, so you will need to match your experience to your searches. Advanced searches allow users to learn specific details about jobs, such as salary range, agency, or individual departments. The website is updated daily, so you will have to be diligent in order to keep up with the postings.

Not all available jobs are posted to **www.USAJOBS.com**, so do not rely on it exclusively. Visit the website of each individual agency and/or department to look for jobs. The specific websites will also provide information on any special programs the department or agency has for students, honors graduates, or new lawyers. The departments and agencies also generally have extensive information on their offices and the type of work they do, which will assist you in deciding whether the agency's or department's work is interesting to you. If you are serious about working for the government, consider using one of the guides that has been published on finding and applying for government jobs. And if you apply for a job, be patient. While you may receive a quick callback for an interview, certain departments may take a while to process and review applications.

The government information in this book is organized by department and agency. Another way to think about your job search is by statute. You can find animal statutes in a report published by the Congressional Research Service (CRS). CRS is a department within the Library of Congress established in 1914 to support Congress with a number of services, including reports, memoranda, and briefings. One of those reports is called *Brief Summaries of Federal Animal Protection Statutes*. The report is prepared for members and committees of Congress and briefly summarizes the approximately 100 animal protection statutes. It also includes statutes that indirectly affect animal protection. For lawyers who are interested in the protection of specific animals or species, this is an excellent way to find the applicable laws along with a brief overview. You can learn more about the law and then further focus your search on the appropriate agencies and departments that administer and enforce the law. For example, the Animal Welfare Act regulates the treatment of animals used in research and exhibitions, transported, and sold or exchanged by dealers. Read the law and investigate its history, its purpose, and the animals and situations to which it applies. You will find that the United States Department of Agriculture and the Animal and Plant Health Inspection Service (APHIS) are responsible for the administration and enforcement of the Animal Welfare Act. These are two places to start a job search—and those two are only the beginning. Also look at other agencies and departments, such as the Environmental Protection Agency, that have a role in enforcement. Then search all of the agencies, departments, and contractors that work for them.

Another law, the Endangered Species Act (ESA) provides for conservation and protection of endangered plants and animals and their habitats. Research on the law will lead you to the U.S. Fish and Wildlife Service, the National Marine Fisheries Service, the Environmental Protection Agency, and the U.S. Department of Justice to start.

Given the sheer size of the federal government and the number and types of jobs available, it is impossible to make generalizations about careers. Salaries are usually acknowledged to be lower than private sector jobs, but higher than some nonprofit jobs. And, there are trade-offs in job security and other benefits. Hours, travel requirements, location, and tracks for advancement vary by job, agency, and department. The hierarchy and work environments vary as well, as with any other large organization or company. A lawyer with the United States Department of Justice may find that he or she works mostly alone in planning and trying cases with little supervision, while a lawyer with the Department of the Interior works mainly in a collaborative setting with significant oversight. Some jobs, simply by their nature, are more stressful than others. Qualifications and experience required are determined by position and are included with each job description on USAJOBS.com, as well as individual departmental and agency job postings.

As you review the following information, think about your personal goals, your timeline, and your career plan. If your main goal is to work in animal protection, keep in mind that governmental issues are often complex. The extent to which a lawyer will have a direct impact on animal protection and conservation will vary. Many of these jobs fall into the "grey area" discussed in the Introduction of this book, or the animal protection factor may be unknown until you start work. For example, a lawyer who files suit on behalf of the government against violators of the ESA will see a direct impact when he or she tries a case. A lawyer with the United States Department of Agriculture who is involved in policy issues may see an impact, but it may be less immediate or direct.

The extent to which government institutions work to protect animals is a controversial issue that will not be addressed in this book. There are numerous agencies within the federal government making any general statement impossible and impractical. There are always multiple interests and politics involved that go beyond animal protection and conservation. The federal departments and agencies that have been established to regulate industries, promulgate rules, and enforce environmental and animal protection laws also have to balance the needs of the public and many other stakeholders. Before you pursue a job with the government, or any organization, the best advice is to do your homework. There is a great deal of information available—pro and con—regarding working for the government, nonprofits, and law firms. And remember, you can always change course.

Government insiders say that there is a great amount of positive work being done in the area of animal protection, and that the best way for animal advocates to see the accomplishments firsthand is to view the efforts from the inside. Attitudes change as public awareness increases and society demands action to punish animal abuse and conserve endangered species and finite natural resources. So, keep an open mind as you review the various agencies and jobs. Only you can decide whether the job and the institution are good fits for you personally and professionally.

A job with the federal government can provide you with a long-term career, a great learning experience, or a stepping-stone to the next phase of your career. There is also a certain stability in working for the government, although in today's world stability is a relative term. Some jobs do come and go with the administration. Governments are bureaucratic by nature, so if you're the entrepreneurial type and like to march to your own drumbeat, be sure to ask about autonomy when interviewing for a position. Some of the key jobs will be located in Washington, D.C., so relocation may be a factor with certain positions. However, there are many government jobs in various locations throughout the country, so do not assume that you will not find the job you want in your city.

The government hires both new lawyers and experienced ones. Read the job descriptions. For law students, there are a number of honors programs and internships at various departments and agencies.

United States Department of Agriculture

One of the largest departments of the federal government is the United States Department of Agriculture (USDA). USDA consists of seventeen agencies and manages 300 programs worldwide. They employ more than 100,000 people and had a 2009 budget of $170.5 billion. On its website, **www.usda.gov**, USDA states that its mission is to "provide leadership on food, agriculture, natural resources, and related issues based on sound public policy, the best available science, and efficient management." Their "Mission Areas" include Farm and Foreign Agricultural Services; Food, Nutrition and Consumer Services; Food Safety; Marketing and Regulatory Programs; Natural Resources and Environment; Research, Education and Economics; and Rural Development. If you are interested in USDA, details can be found on their website, where there are twenty services, offices, and agencies listed with jobs posted on USAJOBS.com.

Part of the work of USDA is in agriculture. The department is extensively involved in the oversight of animals used for food—chickens, cows, and pigs. The agricultural issues they deal with include animal health and diseases, such as mad cow disease and avian flu; animal welfare, including the humane slaughter of farm animals and treatment of animals used in research; economic issues related to food production; aquaculture, including genetic issues, welfare, and imports; conservation, including planning and program management; and production and research. USDA is also involved in issues related to captive animals—commercial breeders, zoos, circuses, and scientific research facilities.

USDA is responsible for the enforcement of the Animal Welfare Act, Horse Protection Act, and other farm animal transport and health standards through its agency, the Animal and Plant Health Inspection Service (APHIS). APHIS is responsible for what it calls the "stewardship" of the animals covered under the Animal Welfare Act. The agency states that it determines "standards of humane care and treatment of animals." The other key agency within USDA is the Food Safety and Inspection Service (FSIS), which is responsible for the implementation and enforcement of laws and regulations governing the humane handling and slaughter of animals used for food. Both agencies have in-house lawyers and other policy, enforcement, and investigative positions where having a law degree would be beneficial in getting hired and in doing the job itself.

Sample Job. An APHIS job posting for a management analyst states that the analyst's duties include the development and administration of "Agency and Program agreements"; drafting and development of recommended policies and guidance for all "domestic and international agreement activities"; and "review, analysis, and commentary on proposed Federal and Departmental agreements, legislative, regulatory, and policy changes." The qualifications for the job include knowledge of domestic and international agreements and related legal processes, plus the ability to review, analyze, and comment on laws.

Office of the General Counsel/USDA

The Office of the General Counsel (OGC) is an independent legal agency within USDA. It provides legal advice and services to the Secretary of Agriculture and all other officials and agencies in the department. All legal services for USDA go through this office. Given USDA's extensive involvement in agriculture, a significant amount of legal work related to animals can be expected to occur. The general counsel is assisted by a deputy general counsel, a senior counselor, six associate general counsels, a director of administration and resource management, and four regional attorneys. The work is carried out in Washington, D.C., four regional offices, and thirteen branch offices around the country.

Work on animal cases would include acting as co-counsel with U.S. attorneys in criminal prosecutions under various animal protection laws and bringing administrative law cases against research facilities, zoos, or circuses found to be in violation of the

Animal Welfare Act. When developing and litigating enforcement actions, OGC lawyers work with government enforcement and investigative specialists who may also be lawyers.

Sample Job. A recent job posting for a trial attorney general with the OGC notes that the lawyer will prepare complicated regulations and drafts of proposed legislation, analyze complaints, advise other lawyers, and try cases.

Department of Commerce

The Department of Commerce's stated mission is to advance economic growth and help make American business more innovative at home and more competitive abroad. The department is involved in trade, technology, entrepreneurship, economic development, and the environment. There are twelve bureaus under the Department of Commerce, most of which relate to business and trade. However, one bureau, the National Oceanic and Atmospheric Administration (NOAA) and its line offices are responsible for the management, conservation, and protection of living marine resources in the United States.

NOAA's National Ocean Service is responsible for maintaining thirteen national marine sanctuaries and one national marine monument. Its primary function is to prevent overfishing and protect marine mammals and other endangered oceanic species. It also manages the Coral Reef Conservation Program, developed to protect coral from the effects of climate change, fishing, and pollution. NOAA Fisheries are directed to promote healthy ecosystems through compliance with the Magnuson-Stevens Act, the ESA, and the Marine Mammal Protection Act. NOAA is also responsible for the protection of 95,439 miles of the country's coast and ecosystems through the Coastal Zone Management Program.

As an example of the work available, NOAA lawyers were involved in the 2010 investigation and prosecution of a man who shot and killed a monk seal on a public beach. Lawyers also act as co-counsel with the Department of Justice in certain wildlife litigation cases, and are involved in the drafting, implementation, and enforcement of regulations. They also litigate administrative cases under the ESA and other wildlife protection laws.

Sample Job. According to the job posting, one of the duties of an NOAA supervisory program analyst is to "direct and oversee the development of ongoing and emerging policy and program planning initiatives within the Office of National Marine Sanctuary (ONMS)." The ONMS serves as the "trustee for the nation's system of marine protected areas, to conserve, protect, and enhance their biodiversity, ecological integrity and cultural legacy." The qualifications require knowledge of legal and policy issues.

Department of Health and Human Services

For those lawyers with a science and/or medical background, the Department of Health and Human Services (HHS) has a number of operating divisions that work directly with animal issues. The Centers for Disease Control and the National Institutes of Health (NIH) are divisions within HHS that are involved in the research and study of the human/animal/environmental health connection. They are "human" health–focused, and jobs with these organizations will likely deal with animals used in scientific research. These agencies (and their lawyers) are involved in research as well as the surrounding policy issues related to the use of animals in research.

The use of animals in research is one of the most controversial issues in animal protection. Some animal welfare advocates believe that it is acceptable to use animals in research to save human lives as long as the animals are treated humanely. Others see any use of animals as unacceptable. While the Animal Welfare Act is intended to protect animals used in research, it does not apply to rats, mice, and birds that make up more than 95 percent of the animals used in research. Another issue that is being increasingly debated is the value of using animals in human medical research. The Physician's Committee for Responsible Medicine is a physician's nonprofit organization that has worked to end animal research through education, arguing that each species is different and researchers can, and have been, misled by results on animals. They have also shown that there are alternatives; today there are few medical schools in the United States and Canada that experiment on animals. In the animal testing realm, the National Research Council issued a report in 2007 on toxicity testing. The report found that revolutions in biology and biotechnology could eliminate toxicity testing on animals due to the superiority of in vitro methods. These debates will no doubt continue as long as animals are used in scientific research.

The Food and Drug Administration (FDA) is another division under HHS that is closely involved with food, drugs, and animal issues. It regulates the food and drugs that are given to animals used for food and to companion animals through its Center for Veterinary Medicine. Lawyers in NIH, FDA, and the Public Health Service, among others, help draft and review regulations administered by those agencies, some of which pertain to research animals. They also help oversee compliance with laws pertaining to animals in research.

Department of Homeland Security

The central mission of the Department of Homeland Security (DHS) is to secure the nation from threats. The department has more than 230,000 employees in areas too numerous to name. DHS came into existence through the consolidation and elimination of a number of government agencies, and today consists of the following departments and organizations: U.S. Customs and Border Protection, U.S. Immigration and Customs Enforcement, U.S. Citizenship and Immigration Services, Transportation Security Administration, Federal Law Enforcement Training Center, Federal Emergency Management Agency (FEMA), Science and Technology Directorate, Office of Cybersecurity and Communications, the U.S. Coast Guard, and the U.S. Secret Service. The department has an extensive website with information on careers, opportunities to do business with the department, and grant opportunities. Go to **www.dhs.gov** for more information on DHS and its activities.

One of the DHS agencies involved in animal issues is FEMA, which has 3,700 employees. FEMA's job is to prepare for disaster and emergency planning, which includes the development, evaluation, and administration of regulations and statutes for handling companion animals in disaster situations. U.S. Customs and Border Protection (CBP) is responsible for controlling what is brought in and out of the country, including the illegal transport of live animals and animal products from endangered species, as well as animals banned for other reasons. In addition to the wildlife aspect,

CBP deals with multiple animal issues, including overseas puppy mills that import dogs illegally into the United States, criminals who attempt to smuggle drugs inside live dogs or other animals, cockfighting roosters shipped illegally into or out of the United States, and the trafficking of endangered wildlife. Lawyers at CBP are often involved in these cases and work up criminal referral packages for the Department of Justice.

Department of Justice

The U.S. Department of Justice (DOJ) was voted one of the best places to work in 2009. The DOJ is responsible for enforcing the laws of the United States. Its mission is to "enforce the law and defend the interests of the United States according to the law; to ensure public safety against threats foreign and domestic; to provide federal leadership in preventing and controlling crime; to seek just punishment for those guilty of unlawful behavior; and to ensure fair and impartial administration of justice for all Americans."

There are numerous agencies and divisions within DOJ. One of the agencies that deals with animal issues is the Environment and Natural Resources Division (ENRD), which is responsible for safeguarding and enhancing the American environment, acquiring and managing public lands and natural resources, and protecting and managing Indian rights and property. ENRD is further segmented into subsections, such as the Wildlife Subsection. The Environmental Crimes Section of ENRD handles criminal wildlife prosecutions.

A legal job with DOJ is a job as a litigator. Their approximately 500 lawyers litigate both civil and criminal cases. In the Wildlife Subsection, lawyers initiate cases against violators of the ESA in civil cases brought by the government. These cases arise from the results of investigations by other departments and agencies, such as the U.S. Fish and Wildlife Service. An investigator will refer a case to DOJ, and the lawyer assigned to the case works with the investigator to prosecute it. On the civil defense side, that same lawyer would defend the United States against a legal challenge brought by an industry or corporation, such as when the government steps in to protect wildlife or a habitat and the industry objects because it wants to destroy the habitat for development or take the water for other uses. Defense cases also include citizen suits related to the

ESA or other wildlife law. Criminal acts related to wildlife laws are also actively investigated and prosecuted by DOJ.

While their work is reviewed, due to the nature of trial work these lawyers generally work autonomously in researching their cases, writing briefs, and preparing for trial. Their hours are dictated in large part by the demands of the cases they are handling.

The DOJ website for jobs is **www.justice.gov/oarm**. In addition to lateral positions for experienced lawyers, they have a number of student programs such as the Attorney General's Honors Program, internships, student temporary employment programs, volunteer programs, and more.

The Federal Bureau of Investigation (FBI) and the U.S. Attorneys' Office are two other departments that litigate animal law cases. The U.S. attorneys play a major role in animal law on the federal side, as they serve as the lead in litigation on criminal cases and work collaboratively with DOJ on some civil cases. Among the types of cases they prosecute are dog fighting cases; Animal Welfare Act criminal violations; ESA prosecutions of smugglers, traffickers, and developers without permits; and Migratory Bird Treaty Act cases against hunters. There are ninety-three U.S. attorneys located throughout the United States, Puerto Rico, the Virgin Islands, Guam, and the Northern Mariana Islands.

Department of the Interior

The United States Department of the Interior (DOI) "protects America's natural resources and heritage, honors our cultures and tribal communities, and supplies the energy to power our future." Its bureaus and offices include the Bureau of Indian Affairs, Bureau of Land Management, Bureau of Reclamation, Minerals Management Service, National Park Service, Office of Surface Mining, U.S. Fish and Wildlife, U.S. Geological Survey, and a number of other offices. There are eleven bureaus, services, and offices that hire under DOI.

Animal-related jobs may fall under several bureaus and offices. The Bureau of Land Management (BLM) administers about 245 million acres of public lands that support a diverse ecosystem of fish, wildlife, and plants. BLM manages livestock grazing and is responsible for the approximately 38,000 wild horses and burros that roam freely on BLM-managed land in certain parts of the Western United States. The bureau states that it manages more wildlife and plant habitats than any other federal or state agency.

The primary DOI agency that impacts animal law is the U.S. Fish and Wildlife Service, which employs its own lawyers. Those lawyers have a similar function to those in the Office of the Solicitor. The Fish and Wildlife Service also has special agents who investigate and prosecute wildlife violations, and hire agents who are also lawyers. By way of example, they conduct undercover investigations of wildlife smugglers, help develop criminal cases based on those investigations, and then testify in the criminal prosecutions.

Office of the Solicitor

The Office of the Solicitor performs the legal work for DOI, manages DOI's Ethics Office and resolves Freedom of Information Act (FOIA) appeals. The Office of the Solicitor employs more than 400 people, 300 of which are lawyers licensed in forty-eight states. Among other responsibilities, these lawyers act as co-counsel to DOJ in wildlife litigation, and are also involved in drafting, implementing, enforcing, and defending wildlife regulations. They also litigate administrative cases such as wildlife smuggling forfeiture actions and civil penalties under the ESA and other wildlife protection laws.

Sample Job. A job posting states that an attorney-advisor would serve as "staff attorney in . . . Albuquerque, New Mexico, providing legal support to the Bureau of Land Management. The legal work includes day-to-day legal advice and counsel, legal research, writing legal opinions[,] . . . assistance to the Department of Justice in judicial litigation and will involve environmental and natural resources laws including FLPMA, NEPA, ESA."

The Office of the Solicitor also has an Honors Attorney Program designed to recruit highly qualified junior lawyers.

Environmental Protection Agency

The Environmental Protection Agency (EPA) is an independent agency of the federal government. It was formed in 1970 in response to public concern about environmental pollution and degradation. The agency's stated mission is to protect human health and to safeguard the natural environment—air, water, and land. It administers or has a hand in administering a significant number of the nation's laws and executive orders, including animal-specific laws such as the ESA and the Marine Protection, Research, and Sanctuaries Act. Other laws it administers, such as the Federal Food, Drug, and Cosmetic Act; Food Quality Protection Act; and Pollution Prevention Act have broad and often direct implications for animals. The Clean Air Act and Clean Water Act have probably the greatest impact on animals, as entities that violate these laws often harm wildlife in the process. Also, because factory farms have violted these laws, EPA has a major initiative to stop factory farm pollution. This in turn affects animals both on and off the farms.

EPA is consistently ranked one of the top places to work. It is headquartered in Washington, D.C., has ten regional offices, and other locations, satellites, and laboratories. EPA lawyers are involved in all of these enforcement actions, and also draft and review regulations pertaining to factory farm pollution and other environmental threats.

Sample Job. A job search found an opening for an attorney advisor (criminal enforcement) who would "work with the Agency's Criminal Investigation Division and the United States Department of Justice . . . to enforce, defend, and implement federal laws and regulations."

State Government

The conviction of Michael Vick, one of the most talented and well-known quarterbacks in football, on felony charges related to dog fighting was a watershed in animal cruelty awareness. Through extensive media coverage, his arrest had a significant impact on the public's awareness and perception of animal cruelty and dog fighting. The media's fascination with the case brought the often disturbing and sordid details and images of the training, torture, and killing of dogs into everyone's living room. The public saw the brutal aspects of dog fighting and its broad criminal reach that may include gambling and other crimes.

Career Profile

Michelle Welch, Assistant Attorney General
Richmond, Virginia

The impact of the Vick case was certainly not lost on Michelle Welch, who has been prosecuting dog fighting cases for years. As assistant attorney general in the Office of the Virginia Attorney General, she was involved in aiding federal prosecutors in the sentencing phase of the Vick case. As a prosecutor and private citizen, Michelle was gratified to see justice served. More importantly, however, she saw how the public awareness that was generated reinforced the importance of investigating and prosecuting cases of animal abuse, dog fighting, and cockfighting in Virginia and throughout the United States.

Michelle had always wanted to be a prosecutor and after law school worked in Richmond, Virginia, as an assistant commonwealth's attorney, later moving up to become deputy commonwealth's attorney. While her career path to prosecutor was planned, Michelle's move into animal law came serendipitously when one of her colleagues asked her to take over her animal cases on a temporary basis. Michelle was at first reluctant to take animal cruelty cases. Seeing animal abuse can be difficult emotionally and Michelle was not sure she wanted to deal with the harsh reality of it. However, she took the cases and found that what she dreaded most—seeing animal abuse—was what made her successful. Seeing animal cruelty energized her to pursue the perpetrators and ensure that the guilty were punished.

Her "temporary" assignment became permanent and Michelle became the animal abuse prosecutor for the City of Richmond in 2000. Historically, animal cases, while crimes like any others, were sometimes neglected or given a low priority. She cared about the cases, took them seriously, thoroughly prepared, and aggressively prosecuted them. Since Michelle began her job as an animal cruelty specialist ten years ago, she has seen the results of her work. Michelle and other lawyers like her have blazed a new path with judges, criminal defense lawyers, and their colleagues for future prosecutors. There is a greater respect for the work she does and there is a new generation of lawyers who do not need convincing that animal cruelty is serious.

When Michelle moved to the state attorney general's office, she took on additional responsibilities, but her animal cases followed her. Today, as an assistant attorney general, she has moved to a big picture role in animal cruelty prosecutions. She serves as special prosecutor in Virginia's animal cases, but also advises law enforcement and prosecutors throughout the state on how to investigate and prosecute dog fighting, cockfighting, and animal cruelty cases.

Michelle is happiest when she is in the courtroom. Whether in front of a jury or a judge, she is energized by the legal process. Her days are never the same, and consist of preparing for trial and fielding questions from lawyers or animal control officers regarding their animal cases. Her preparation for an animal cruelty or dog fighting case is largely the same as with any other crime, with one key difference: the victim is an animal. An animal can never point out the abuser or make a statement. Michelle must build her cases around animal control officers, any witnesses, available forensic and other evidence, and the opinions of veterinarians and other experts. And she always over-prepares, never underestimating the ability of a criminal defense lawyer to come up with something new. And in a legal world where complaints of incivility among lawyers are increasing, she notes that it helps to be friendly.

Through her extensive experience Michelle has become an expert on animal law, conducting training sessions not only for prosecutors and law enforcement, but also for animal control officers and other lawyers. She teaches animal law at the University of Richmond, speaks regularly on animal law issues, and serves on various boards and committees related to animal law and animal welfare.

Michelle advises law students who want to prosecute animal cruelty to look for summer internships in city district attorney offices. Internships provide valuable first-hand experience and allow the prosecutors who work there to evaluate students' work. As for animal cruelty cases, Michelle counsels students to determine quickly whether or not they have the mental strength to put animal abuse cases away and leave them behind. If not, it's best to think about another career. Working as a prosecutor is just one career in animal protection. If it is the right one, set a course in law school to be a litigator. There is much students can do in law school to prepare for trial work. For a lawyer already working as a prosecutor, take animal law cases. It's the first step in becoming an expert.

Every state has laws against animal cruelty, dog fighting, cockfighting, and other animal-related crimes. Small towns and rural areas generally have fewer resources and must prioritize their efforts. It means that less attention is generally devoted to animal cruelty and that fewer opportunities exist to practice in these areas. However, it does not mean that opportunities do not exist. The reality is that the more society learns about animal cruelty, the more important it becomes to stop it. Empirical evidence is proving what many working in animal law already know—that there is a relationship between animal cruelty and human violence, family violence, illegal drugs, gambling, and more. These findings mean that every community must begin to seriously address animal abuse. It is no longer just about animals.

"You make your career what you want it to be. You shape your own destiny."

At the Local Level

One city that takes animal abuse seriously is Houston, Texas, in Harris County. Belinda Smith is the chief prosecutor of the Animal Cruelty Section in the Harris County District Attorney's Office. In addition to being the lead prosecutor in animal cruelty cases, she works to help advance state and county legislation related to animal fighting and trains and advises law enforcement and animal control personnel throughout the state on recognizing and investigating animal-related crimes.

Career Profile

Belinda Smith, Chief Prosecutor
Harris County District Attorney's Office
Houston, Texas

When asked to define her job, Belinda states unequivocally that she is a prosecutor. She has taken an oath to seek justice. While passionate about animal welfare, she is quick to note that her role as an animal lawyer is secondary and is defined by the relevant local, state, and federal laws related to animals. When laws affecting animals change, her role as an animal lawyer changes; she understands that animal law does not always mean animal protection.

Houston's focus on animal cruelty started in 2006 when Belinda asked permission to handle all of the animal cruelty cases. She had been concerned with the inconsistencies she saw in the way animal cruelty cases were investigated and prosecuted. The cases were randomly assigned and different prosecutors had varying opinions on animal abuse and how the cases should be handled. She convinced her boss that she could handle the cases in addition to her current workload, while bringing greater consistency to the way the cases were investigated and prosecuted. Her boss agreed and Belinda started that year with forty-two cases.

The good news is that once law enforcement learned that Belinda was handling all of the cases, they stepped up their animal cruelty investigations. The bad news is that their efforts showed that animal cruelty was a serious problem. Two years after taking on forty-two cases, Belinda was handling more than 200 cases a year. Then in 2009, newly elected District Attorney Patricia R. Lykos created the state's first and only animal cruelty section. The section consisted of two prosecutors and an investigator; Belinda was named the chief of the section. During this time, her section helped plan and implement "Operation Dead Game," an undercover sting operation that infiltrated one of the largest dog fighting rings in the country at the time. The investigation resulted in the prosecution of more than 100 offenders for dog fighting, narcotics, and fencing of stolen property.

Belinda knew that in order to be successful, her department had to be credible. The Animal Cruelty Section was new, not only in Houston but also in general, and not all of her colleagues were supportive of channeling limited resources into animal crimes. While everyone knows that animal cruelty is a crime, not everyone believes it should be a priority. However, Belinda more than rose to the occasion with the success of Operation Dead Game and her tireless efforts to market both her department's accomplishments and the importance of prosecuting animal cruelty. She now sees attitudes changing as evidence mounts that people who abuse animals are likely to commit other crimes, including violence against people. There is a human cost of neglecting these crimes that is being proven repeatedly.

A "day in the life" of an animal cruelty prosecutor is much the same as a day in the life of any other prosecutor. Belinda goes to court in the mornings and meets with defense attorneys on plea negotiations. Most of her cases do not go to trial. In the afternoons she spends time working on her cases. Given some of the unique evidentiary issues that arise in animal cases, her department takes its own intake calls. Belinda emphasizes that prosecuting animal-related crimes can be difficult emotionally, regardless of whether you consider yourself an animal advocate. Some cases involve horrific instances of animal cruelty, but as a lawyer and prosecutor you must be able to deal with the realities in a professional manner. While some cases still get to her, she has learned when to take a break or bring in another person. Her job has many rewards, but it is not "warm and fuzzy." Challenges of the job include the general frustrations that come with being a prosecutor, but a particular challenge in animal cruelty cases is evidentiary support, which can be scant or missing.

Belinda welcomes the assistance of law students who wish to volunteer in her section. She speaks at law schools in the area and uses the opportunity to choose the interns that will assist her department. She looks for students who want to be prosecutors. Beyond that she does not require any specific credentials. Many interns who work for her are interested in animal welfare, but Belinda cautions against straying too far from the mainstream as a prosecutor. Credibility is key, and animal cruelty prosecutors need the respect of law enforcement, other lawyers, judges, and the communities they serve. Negative perceptions still exist and can undermine the ultimate goal of punishing those who commit criminal acts of animal cruelty.

Belinda's interns get hands-on experience in animal cruelty investigations and prosecutions and will quickly determine whether or not Belinda's career path is right for them. They are spared nothing and go to court every morning, sit in on meetings with defense lawyers in plea bargains, and visit crime scenes. They see nuances among various judges and how they can affect the outcomes of cases.

After working exclusively in animal cruelty for the last four years, Belinda believes that every city needs an animal cruelty specialty division in order to be more effective and efficient in prosecuting these cases. Based on her experience, she believes that the public is more than ready to support it. As a testament to the growing interest in fighting animal cruelty, news reporters *and* law enforcement show up for Belinda's January "Crime Stoppers" press conference. She believes it is only a matter of time before all cities see the many benefits of having an animal cruelty specialist.

In-House Counsel

There are lawyers who prefer working as in-house counsel rather than in a traditional role as a lawyer in a law firm or other setting. Often considered choice legal positions, the general opinion is that in-house lawyers encounter less stress, work fewer hours, and have greater job security than lawyers with firms. In certain situations this may be true, although in today's employment environment it is unwise to make any assumptions about stability, work load, or security.

In-house lawyers are often hired from the law firms that have been servicing a company's accounts; the lawyers know the company and the industry, eliminating an often steep learning curve. If the company is large enough, it may have a team of lawyers, including junior-level positions, along with outside counsel hired for specific cases.

It would be stretching the definition of animal lawyer if I suggested that working as in-house counsel for an animal-related industry is practicing animal law. In-house lawyers, even those who work for humane organizations, deal with legal issues involving employment, securities, real estate, criminal, and consumer law. Animal law is probably rarely in the mix, even for companies providing animal-related products and services. Nonetheless, I have included this section for several reasons. As indicated earlier in the book, my goal is to include as many options as possible, with the knowledge that some jobs have more tenuous connections to animals and the law than others. I do not want to forgo the chance that a job scenario may lead someone to an "aha" moment and an ideal career.

Another reason is that statistics show that lawyers and other professionals entering the workforce today will not retire with the companies that originally hire them. A job may be one stop along a career path, not a final career. The experience gained from a position with an animal-related company may equip you with valuable knowledge that meets your long-term objectives or provides a stepping-stone to the next stage in your career.

For-Profits and Nonprofits

Finally, I have included working in for-profit environments in order to illustrate a few key differences between nonprofit and for-profit companies. While there are similarities, and some large nonprofits operate like corporations, their purposes differ. Most humane organizations and animal advocacy groups have opted to be governed as 501(c)(3) charities under Internal Revenue Code section

501. This means they were formed around a charitable purpose, in this case animal advocacy, which is a requirement for 501(c)(3) status. This designation from the U.S. Internal Revenue Service (IRS) means the organization has satisfied the IRS requirements that its goals and activities are intended to provide charitable services to the public, not to private individuals. In exchange for being a charity, nonprofits receive a number of financial benefits. Primarily, donors to the organization receive a tax deduction, helping the nonprofit to raise funds.

The federal and state laws and IRS rules and regulations governing charities and for-profit companies are complex, but there are a few relevant distinctions that should be mentioned. A charitable organization is under a constraint regarding the distribution of its earnings. While it can operate as a business and pay employee salaries and earn "profits," those profits cannot be distributed to shareholders, board members, or other interested individuals. The money must be reinvested in the nonprofit (or another qualifying nonprofit) to further its charitable purposes. Nonprofits are also under constraints regarding their ability to lobby and participate in the political process. (See the section on "Lobbying" in Chapter 6 for more information on nonprofits and political activity.)

In contrast, for-profit companies are recognized as being in business to make money—for their shareholders, their employees and officers, and/or their owners. That is their primary purpose and the reason for their existence. They pay a price in the form of taxes and other obligations that nonprofit organizations do not. They must be competitive in their markets and usually have to pay higher salaries if they want to recruit and retain the best employees. The employee mindset is on productivity and efficiency in order to obtain the highest return on investments.

Because of their different purposes and financial structures, the corporate cultures at nonprofits and for-profits will naturally be different. The culture of the nonprofit is centered on the organization's charitable mission. While the financial bottom line is important, it is important not because of an obligation to provide shareholders a better return on their investment, but because the money goes to further the organization's charitable causes. The employees who work in nonprofits do so with the "nonprofit" mindset that their efforts are directed toward a charitable purpose. A 501(c)(3) organization is required to keep salaries in line with others in similar jobs. And while those salaries may be high for certain positions, an organization may choose to keep salaries low in order to have more funds to spend on their programs. Income is not the prime motivator for people seeking work in the nonprofit area.

As for charitable endeavors, some for-profit companies are considered good corporate citizens in that they contribute to charitable causes, but it is not a legal requirement. Many corporations do so because it is good business. The public looks favorably on companies that give back to the community, and that favorable view translates into greater sales and increases to the bottom line. For charities, corporate support can be invaluable if it does not conflict with the nonprofit's mission. However, a corporation will be unlikely to fund a charitable enterprise at the expense of the financial well-being of the corporation. So keep in mind the for-profit and nonprofit cultures as you think about working as in-house counsel.

Retail and Manufacturing Companies

Statistics show that Americans spend billions of dollars a year on their companion animals for food, toys, clothing, veterinary care, boarding, and more. These numbers are not lost on retailers as animal-related businesses, large and small, continue to proliferate. For those lawyers with an MBA or business background, working as in-house counsel for a retailer or manufacturer of animal-related products and/or services may be the right career path.

There are numerous local and national retailers, from the local shop down the street to international companies with worldwide locations. Retailers provide numerous products and services—everything from boarding, grooming, training, and adoptions to toys, food, beds, and shampoo. One such international company is PetSmart, which has more than 1,000 stores in the United States and Canada; they provide services for care and sell supplies including food, toys, and equipment. Careers are posted on their website at careers.petsmart.com.

PetSmart was instrumental in starting PetSmart Charities, an independent 501(c)(3) nonprofit organization. Its stated mission is to "improve the quality of life for all pets by creating and supporting programs that save the lives of homeless pets and promote healthy relationships between people and pets." The work of the nonprofit includes partnering with and supporting animal welfare organizations across North America.

On the manufacturing side, companies produce crates, toys, beds, food, and numerous other products for animals. Businesses vary, with some choosing to narrowly focus on products such as dog chews or toys. Some may manufacture and sell their products. These companies may also work with rescue groups, shelters, and humane societies.

These are examples of the many types of companies that provide goods and services to the animal industry. These companies cater primarily to owners of companion animals, but there are also industries built around horses, exotic pets, or fish.

If a career as in-house counsel for a large company is not a good fit, consider the many smaller companies that could use the services of a lawyer. While the work may start with pro bono or reduced fees, you can build credibility and expertise with the organization and perhaps help build it into a larger one. Look around and you will find trainers, boarders, groomers, pet stores, and even pet psychologists who may need legal services.

As mentioned earlier, much of the work of the in in-house lawyer may have little to do with animal protection. However, one relevant legal focus for these companies is animal safety, which cannot be compromised. The melamine contamination of pet food that surfaced in 2007 and the subsequent litigation are reminders that people care deeply about their animals and will hold those responsible for their injuries accountable. So check out the company and determine whether working in a for-profit corporate environment is compatible with your career goals. While there may not be a direct connection to animal welfare, you may make a difference through the advice you give and the work you do while gaining valuable experience.

Within the for-profit world, there is also a difference between a publicly traded company and a privately held one. Publicly traded companies, those listed on a stock exchange, are indebted financially to their shareholders. Their operations and finances will be relatively open and transparent. Private companies answer to their owners, who have greater flexibility in deciding whether to share financial and other information about the company. Whatever form the company takes, do your homework to learn as much as possible about the company's animal culture and management attitudes.

6 Nonlegal Jobs, Animals, and the Law

Not every law school graduate will work in the traditional practice of law, meaning working in a firm or in some capacity as a lawyer representing clients. Some students attend law school with no intention of practicing. They want a juris doctor because it will be valuable to them in other professions. Students may also plan to work in a firm but find more interesting nonlegal jobs. And, given the intense competition for fewer legal jobs in today's market, graduates may decide to take a nonlegal job out of necessity.

There are also lawyers who choose to leave the field, sometimes after a year or even twenty years. Burnout, disenchantment with the profession, or perhaps a more exciting option can motivate lawyers to make career changes. If they do not want to totally abandon years of hard work and knowledge, they will look for jobs that allow them to use some of their legal skills.

As indicated earlier, as more law schools offer animal law courses, more students want to practice, resulting in more lawyers vying for limited positions. The situation is complicated by the fact that in animal law, the traditional positions—such as staff attorneys for humane organizations and firms—are few, making them very competitive. Therefore, lawyers who want to leave a practice, are not set on practicing, or are more focused on working in animal protection than in a legal setting will have more options to consider.

The following career paths cover broad areas, from teaching to lobbying to starting a nonprofit. In keeping with the recurrent theme of this book, read ahead with an open and creative mind.

Animal Law in Academia

As of November 2010, the Animal Legal Defense Fund reported that 121 law schools in Canada (3) and the United States (118) offered animal law courses. The number and types of classes taught are not included, but one can assume that most of the classes are survey courses (although some schools offer additional classes, such as wildlife law and animal law litigation). The numbers translate into more than 100 adjunct and full-time professors teaching animal law in the United States. The statistics are impressive and illustrate how far the field has come in its development. However, it also means that animal law is still a nascent discipline in academia and that there is still growth potential and opportunity. With approximately 250 law schools across the country, more than half have yet to add animal law to their curricula.

If you are considering law school with a focus on animal law, research the programs at the various schools that offer classes. Look for clinics, a variety of classes, how long the program has been in existence, and other offerings.

Animal law received a major boost in 2004 when Bob Barker, long-time host of the television show *The Price Is Right*, gave a number of $1 million endowments for the study of animal law to several law schools, including Stanford Law School, Columbia Law School, Duke University School of Law, and the UCLA School of Law. The endowment fund began in 2001 when Pearson Television, owner of *The Price Is Right*, wanted to honor Barker for his thirty years on the show. Barker convinced Pearson to make a $500,000 donation to Harvard Law School, and Harvard used the money to establish the Bob Barker Endowment Fund for the Study of Animal Rights.

George Washington University Law School held its first animal law seminar in 2001, and now offers an animal law program with the goal of graduating young lawyers who will be among a group of lawyers, judges, and legislators addressing animal cruelty and neglect and promoting and protecting the broader interests of animals through the law. Under the direction of full-time faculty member Joan Schaffner, the program includes two seminars and various projects such as the Animal Welfare Project, which seeks to raise awareness of animal welfare issues through research, reporting, and legislation, and the Animal Law Lawyering Project, which provides students internship opportunities at a variety of humane organizations involved in litigation, legislation, and educational campaigns affecting animals. The program hosts speakers and conferences on a variety of animal law topics and has drafted reports and legislation to enhance the protection of animals in Washington, D.C.

Lewis & Clark Law School in Portland, Oregon is one of the pioneers in animal law. They offer a specialty in animal law, and to date it is the only comprehensive program in the country designed for students who are interested in practicing animal law. The school also runs a Center for Animal Law Studies in collaboration with the Animal Legal Defense Fund. The Center is an "animal law think tank" and the umbrella organization for their animal law program. Among other activities, the school houses the nation's premier Animal Law Clinic; offers multiple animal law courses, including advanced courses; has the nation's only Summer Intensive Animal Law Program, which began in 2004; holds an annual conference, The Animal Law Conference at Lewis & Clark, which began in 1993; presents the annual National Animal Law Competitions at Harvard Law School, which began in 2004; and is home to the *Animal Law Review*, published since 1994.

Several schools publish animal law journals. The students of Lewis & Clark Law School publish *Animal Law*; the *Stanford Journal of Animal Law and Policy* is an online-only journal; and the *Journal of Animal Law* is a publication of the Michigan State University College of Law. These journals contribute to legal scholarship in animal law, which is critical to its continued development as a legal discipline.

Michigan State University College of Law publishes legal articles, cases, news, statutes, and information on animal law throughout the country on its extensive website, the Animal Legal and Historical Web Center (**www.animallaw.info**). The Center provides information at no cost, allowing lawyers and researchers to freely access cases and research that might otherwise be unavailable. The website is the brainchild of David Favre, professor of law at Michigan State, who continues to manage the site.

Career Profile

David Favre, Professor of Law
Michigan State University College of Law
East Lansing, Michigan

David Favre's work in animal law spans thirty years. He is one of those rare individuals who has not only witnessed the growth of the animal protection movement, but has lived it. He has made significant contributions to animal welfare and the law and continues to do so today.

David's original interest in law school was environmental law, which he continues to teach today. After graduating, he and a fellow student started an environmental law practice. They quickly decided that the timing was not right, and David changed his focus from practicing law to teaching it. An academic career would allow him to stay connected to environmental law through teaching and research, as well as pursue his other interests to a greater degree. He was hired by Michigan State University College of Law in 1976 where he is a professor of law.

While David had been aware of animal issues as part of his environmental work, his true exposure to the field of animal law started with his first law review article in 1979. The article's focus on wildlife rights earned him an invitation to speak at one of the early animal law conferences in Brooklyn, New York. At the conference he met the lawyers who would later collaborate and form the Attorneys for Animal Rights, the early incarnation of the Animal Legal Defense Fund (ALDF). He joined the group and went on to serve as a director on the ALDF board for twenty-two years, where he helped guide the organization in its mission to end animal cruelty.

One of his responsibilities with ALDF was to play an active role in international animal law. He enhanced his knowledge of wildlife law and attended meetings of the members of the Convention in the International Trade in Endangered Species of Wild Fauna and Flora (CITES). The results of his work include a book on wildlife law, *Wildlife: Cases, Laws, and Policy*, and his co-founding of the Species Survival Network (SSN), an "international coalition of non-governmental organizations committed to the promotion, enhancement, and strict enforcement of CITES." SSN's work continues today with the goal of preventing the over-exploitation of animals and plants due to international trade.

In the early 1990s, the animal protection movement was gaining momentum. ALDF generated greater awareness and support for its mission, and the overall strategic thinking in animal law became more sophisticated. ALDF was actively litigating cases and HSUS was focused on legislation. Animal law classes were popping up at law schools around the country and students began to take classes not simply out of curiosity, but because they were interested in working in the field.

During that time, David was teaching, writing, and speaking extensively on animal protection. His publications include an animal law textbook and a dozen animal law books, chapters, and articles covering animal law and international animal issues.

As he saw the practice of animal law grow, he saw a need for a central source of law and cases. Many lawyers did not have the financial resources to subscribe to legal research services, so he established a free legal resource on a website for animal law practitioners, students, and other advocates interested in the field. With some financial support from ALDF and his law school, the Animal Legal and Historical Web Center website was launched and remains the most extensive free resource for animal-related news, cases, laws, and articles. The site is continuously updated. David recently received a grant from the Arcus Foundation to enhance the site with research and information on great apes.

David no longer serves on the board of ALDF, but his efforts in international animal law continue. In 2004, he helped organize and was a featured speaker at the First Global Conference on the Legal Status of Animal Welfare Issues, a groundbreaking international event that hosted speakers from eight countries. The impact of the conference did not end with its conclusion, as a global network of lawyers and professors remain and continue to communicate and collaborate with each other on international animal issues. David travels throughout the world to countries such as China, Japan, Kenya, Spain, and New Zealand, speaking on animal law issues and assisting countries in their efforts to draft animal protection legislation and fight animal abuse. In a number of places, David has seen their efforts proceed at a faster pace than those in the United States.

Today, David's career is focused on teaching and communicating his ideas on animals and the law through writing and speaking engagements. While it would be impossible to recreate his exact career path, David's work serves as an example that opportunities still exist to teach, speak, and contribute to the scholarship and discourse in animal law.

Teaching Animal Law as an Adjunct Professor

Law schools hire full-time professors and educators. Contract workers, referred to as *adjuncts* in academia, are hired to teach a specific course or courses; this is the extent of their work. They receive none of the benefits of full-time employees. Most adjuncts already have full-time jobs and are hired because of their expertise in the subjects the school wants to offer.

Animal law is one of the specialties in which many law schools hire adjuncts or lecturers. The full-time professors may not have the necessary knowledge, since it is a relatively new field, or may not have an academic interest. Several of the lawyers profiled in this book are adjunct professors. They had the experience, along with an interest in teaching and promoting animal law as a discipline. Policies and procedures may differ slightly, but most law schools have curriculum committees. Lawyers interested in teaching will need to submit a proposal for the course that includes the adjunct's credentials, a description of the course, a syllabus, the students' requirements, etc.

Adjunct professors are generally not interested in joining the faculty of a law school. They may not have the credentials necessary for a tenure-track job in academia, and they are not hired as full-time professors (though situations do arise where adjuncts leave their practices for full-time jobs in academia). However, an adjunct position can enhance your credentials and provide a way to enjoy teaching, promoting animal law, and interacting with students.

The Tenure Track

Securing a tenure-track position as a professor is a much more challenging pursuit than being hired as a lecturer or adjunct. David Favre cites factors such as shrinking law school budgets and increased competition for fewer jobs that make finding an academic career difficult today. An animal law focus is particularly difficult, if not impossible, unless the school has an animal law program. Anyone looking for a full-time position as a professor must have primary interests and expertise in other legal fields.

For students who want to enhance their credentials for high-level policy work in government, specialization, or academia, law schools offer degrees beyond the juris doctor. The LLM, or Master of Laws, is one such advanced degree offered at many law schools. Additionally, some schools offer degree programs beyond the LLM for aspiring academics. However, the degree is only one component. The highly qualified candidates that David Favre is seeing at Michigan State and in academia overall have the following credentials:

- Academic excellence in law school. A candidate's credentials start with a review of his or her academic performance in law school. Usually, their law school is ranked in the top twenty.
- One or two years of experience as a clerk for a judge. A clerkship with a prominent judge is a resume builder in addition to providing a valuable and unique legal education.
- Five years of experience with a large law firm. Beyond law school, a lawyer must have a work record to promote. A candidate who has had a career with a large firm brings prestige to the law school and valuable experience to impart to students.
- Two published law review articles. Publishing is important not only while working in academia, but in getting hired in academia.
- Legal expertise that is in demand at the law school. This requirement is mostly beyond the candidate's control. However, administrators and academics tend to agree that animal law is too new to make a favorable impact as a primary area of interest. Candidates should research trends in the law and in law schools to determine evolving areas of the law on which to focus. Animal law can be a secondary interest.

The bar is quite high, and lawyers without these credentials will need to compensate with other achievements. Perhaps you have published a book, making two law review articles less important. Maybe you have built a successful solo firm, surpassing what you would have accomplished as a member of a firm. Also consider any volunteer work where you may have contributed to the financial and legal successes of a nonprofit organization.

There are many benefits that come with a position as a tenured professor. Teaching is an enjoyable experience on many fronts. If you enjoy teaching and writing, it is the perfect job. Once tenured, your job is secure in that you have the freedom to express your ideas without the fear of reprisals that exists in other jobs. A career in academia also allows the time and flexibility to travel, conduct research, write, and pursue other interests.

Nevertheless, teaching is not for everyone. The salaries are generally lower than those of practicing lawyers, and many lawyers enjoy the fast pace and intensity of the practice of law. The law school environment lacks mobility in that once tenured, it is a bit more difficult to move. If you are hired in a city you do not like, you may have fewer options.

Other Academic Pursuits

The study of animals is not limited to the law school environment. If a career as a law school professor or adjunct is not a possibility but you want to teach, consider other schools. There are community colleges and universities where you can market your skills and talents and educate in animal law and protection. For example, New York University offers a minor in animal studies to its undergraduates as part of its Animal Studies Initiative.

Investigate the schools in your area to see where animal welfare or animal studies might fit into the curriculum. Be creative and look for ways to forge new paths. If student demand is there, schools will offer it.

Tap into Your Creativity

Today the expansive media world of the Internet, multiple cable channels, e-books, movies, and radio has produced many successes and offers expanded opportunities for new creative talent to enter the market.

Writing

For early advocates, the animal rights movement started with the book *Animal Liberation* by Peter Singer, an Australian philosopher. First published in 1975, the book brought to light the cruel treatment and suffering of animals in scientific research facilities and factory farms. Considered by many to be the bible of the animal rights movement, it has maintained its relevance and is now in its third printing.

The public's interest in animals continues to grow, evidenced by the steady stream of animal-related books that enter the market. Mainstream publishing houses are accepting works of fiction and non-fiction about animal intelligence, animals used for food, the human/animal bond, and our treatment of animals. Their decisions are paying off as books such as *Marley and Me* (also a movie) by journalist John Grogan, *Alex and Me* by Irene Pepperberg, and *Merle's Door* by Ted Kerasote hit the bestseller lists. Books that educate and inform, such as *Animals in Translation* by Temple Grandin have found their way into the mainstream market and the bestseller list. Lawyers-turned-authors such as John Grisham and Scott Turow are proof that a writing career is possible. Scott Turow wrote *One L: The Turbulent Story of a First Year at Harvard Law School* while he was still in law school. More than thirty years later, the book remains in publication.

Where there was previously a scarcity of scholarly writing on animals and the law, articles and books on animal issues such as ethics, law, philosophy, and sociology are now easily found, and the selections are increasing. The ABA Tort Trial and Insurance Practice Section has published books on wildlife law, litigating animal disputes, and dangerous dog issues. Philosophers and professors such as Martha C. Nussbaum and Bernard Rollin, as well as lawyer, professor, and legal scholar Cass R. Sunstein, have published books and articles on animal law and ethics.

There are numerous books, guides, and classes on how to write a book, find a publisher, and get published. Publishers are usually specific in their requirements for the submission of proposals and manuscripts, so if you have an idea, check various publishers' requirements and follow the rules.

Publishing has changed with the advent of new technology. While many readers still relish the feel of a printed book or newspaper, the electronic reader is making progress and has reengineered the business of publishing and reading. E-books can be downloaded quickly and hundreds of books can be stored on one device. Electronic publishing now offers the novice writer an easy way to self-publish his or her work. For example, Kindle®, the electronic reader by Amazon, offers a method of self-publishing through its Digital Text Platform (DTP).

If writing a book is too daunting a task, consider starting with articles, essays, op-ed pieces, poetry, or short stories for magazines, newspapers, or online publications. Have a great idea for a collection of works? Assemble a group of experts to do the writing and serve as editor. Animal law still offers many publishing opportunities. Lawyers with a love of writing become journalists, freelance writers, and experts in their fields. Perhaps your city's newspaper needs a correspondent on animal law issues.

Television and Movies

Animals have been the stars of films and television programs for years. Lassie was a staple of childhoods in the 1960s, and animals continue to be featured in television in more ways than ever. In the past, animals used in entertainment were more easily exploited. Today there are stricter standards and greater oversight. The National Geographic Channel has produced documentaries that entertain without disturbing the animal's existence or nature's balance. They have educated us on the habits and unique characteristics of the many species with which we share our world. *The Dog Whisperer* with Cesar Millan is a testament to our love of dogs and our desire to have them in our lives. For the lawyer with a creative bent and an idea, a documentary or television show may launch a new career.

Animal films and documentaries cover broad subjects, from topics such as the dolphin harvests in Japan in the movie *The Cove*, to poignant films such as *March of the Penguins* by award-winning director Luc Jacquet. These films serve to educate on the intelligence and unique lives of animals and draw attention to some of the harsh practices related to our use of them. The development and production of these films show no signs of abating. Greater awareness of what many consider the unacceptable treatment of animals used for food, in entertainment, and even as companions, has generated calls for change. Those in the field of animal law understand how the media affects public opinion and its advantages and disadvantages in the context of the work they do. Visual media can be extremely effective in stirring emotions and prompting action where other efforts fail.

Finally, if you are not destined to write the great animal law novel or produce the next award-winning documentary, consider the career of an entertainment lawyer, who advises the media industry on its legal obligations related to the use of animals.

Become a Lobbyist

For lawyers who want to use their legal training and expertise in a different but related career, becoming a lobbyist is one possibility. A lobbyist advocates a position in an effort to influence legislation and affect public policy. Lobbying is as old as politics itself; every citizen has the right to participate in the political process through lobbying his or her elected representatives at every level of government. Citizens with common interests form grassroots advocacy groups and lobby their representatives on political issues that affect them. These groups are often vocal and determined and can be effective in influencing their legislators on a variety of issues. These individual citizens and groups usually lobby because they have strong views or personal stakes in the outcomes of laws being considered. They generally lobby on behalf of their own interests, not for other organizations or companies or for compensation. The benefit they seek is a legislator's vote that agrees with their views.

In contrast, a professional lobbyist is a person who is paid to advocate for a client's position. Businesses and organizations employ lobbyists to educate and inform decision-makers on issues in which they have vested interests, monetarily and otherwise.

Like other professionals, lobbyists may work in small- or medium-sized firms or in solo practice settings. They have a number of different clients who have hired them for their knowledge and their one-on-one access to federal and state lawmakers, government officials, and other key influencers who can act on that client's needs. Whether the lobbyist has a personal interest in an issue is usually irrelevant, although he or she must have relevant knowledge.

Some lobbyists work for organizations on a full-time, in-house basis. An in-house lobbyist is someone who is devoted full-time to the organization's business and experiences first-hand the ongoing needs of that organization and the industry. The in-house lobbyist has a greater interest in the long-term success of the company and the laws that affect it, as opposed to an outside lobbyist, who is focused on the current project's success.

While the corrupt practices of a few high-profile lobbyists have caused some to malign the profession, a general denunciation is unwarranted. Lawmakers cannot possibly know everything about every issue, and lobbyists serve important roles in educating and raising awareness of the impact of certain courses of action. Lobbyists research and analyze legislation, study the regulatory environment, and provide in-depth analyses and information that would otherwise be unavailable.

Historically, animal welfare groups have not been as active in lobbying for animal-related legislation as other industries. In the past, many of these organizations did not have the financial means to hire lobbyists and directed the money they did have into direct care for animals. Moreover, nonprofit groups with tax-exempt status under Internal Revenue Code section 501(c)(3) cannot expend a "substantial" part of their activities on influencing legislation. Having no clear definition from the IRS of "substantial," most groups avoided any lobbying for fear of losing their charitable status. However, nonprofits can now choose to be regulated by a more definitive expenditure test that allows them to spend certain amounts on lobbying without a penalty or threat to their tax-exempt status. Section 501(h) of the Internal Revenue Code permits organizations to opt out of the "no substantial part" test and be governed by specific rules. It gives these organizations the ability to participate in the political process within established limitations. Another option for animal welfare groups is to form what is known as a 501(c)(4) organization, which provides fewer benefits than the 501(c)(3), but allows greater flexibility in lobbying. Donations to a 501(c)(4) organization are not tax deductible.

While many lobbyists have prior experience in public service or certain industry sectors, this experience is not required to become a lobbyist or even to be a good one. A good lobbyist has a thorough knowledge and understanding of the client's business and goals, as well as what government can do to further or hinder those goals. He or she must also know how to package and communicate that message to legislators in a way that benefits all parties—the legislator, his or her constituents, the public, and, most importantly, the company. A legal education and related experience provide an excellent foundation in knowledge of the law and the workings of government. This knowledge can be invaluable when interpreting legislation and its consequences.

The salary ranges from low to very high, depending on the lobbyist's credentials and the resources of the clients who engage their services. Some contract lobbyists can demand large hourly rates based on their experience, knowledge, access, and success rates. An in-house lobbyist will likely be salaried, with the amount dependent on the organization's resources and the employee's experience. In general, the greater the experience and the bigger the client, the greater the salary potential and the hourly rate.

Lobbyists have to be located where the government transacts business when in session, whether in Washington, D.C. or the various state capitals. However, while it is generally convenient to live where you work, lobbying offers some flexibility. Some lobbyists travel to different cities around the country, making a hometown irrelevant.

Career Profile

Ledy Van Kavage, Senior Legislative Attorney
Best Friends Animal Society
Kanab, Utah

One such traveling lobbyist is Ledy Van Kavage, a lawyer and lobbyist based in Collinsville, Illinois. Ledy is senior legislative attorney for Best Friends Animal Society, a nonprofit located in Kanab, Utah. Best Friends is a nonprofit organization that runs the nation's largest sanctuary for abused and abandoned animals and works toward a goal of virtually eliminating the number of unwanted pets in the United States.

Ledy's work takes her all over the country. During state legislative sessions, she travels to various state capitols where she walks the halls reconnecting with people she knows and introducing herself to those she doesn't. She works behind the scenes, testifies at hearings, and works one-on-one with senators, representatives, other lobbyists, and stakeholders who can assist her in promoting the goals and objectives of Best Friends. As an individual she attends fundraisers to show support for lawmakers who support humane legislation, as well as fundraisers for those who remain to be convinced.

When legislators are not in session, Ledy monitors the legal landscape for animals. She watches off-year federal and state activities, reviews relevant case law, conducts legal analyses, and absorbs the news that will assist her in planning a legislative strategy. She drafts bills, directs media efforts and public relations campaigns, and organizes grassroots advocacy. Ledy also volunteers her time in support of animal welfare and speaks regularly to share her knowledge with other groups that want to participate in the political process for the benefit of animals. She is chair of the ABA Tort, Trial and Insurance Practice Section Animal Law Committee for 2011–12.

According to Ledy, mandatory traits of the successful lobbyist include tenacity, good social skills, and a talent for public speaking. It is generally not a team activity and requires self-motivation and the ability to work independently. Lobbying is not a nine-to-five job, as legislative sessions often run into the evening. Fundraisers are also typically evening events, and travel may be a requirement. But the job is never boring.

"Politics is not a spectator sport. Business, insurance, and agriculture interests have packs of lobbyists roaming the halls. Animal welfare organizations are finally grasping the importance of having lobbyists at the capitol to be the voice of the animals. Getting a humane bill signed creates immediate change. I know of no greater calling."

By working as a lobbyist for an animal welfare organization, you can have a direct effect on the laws that impact animals. It may mean long hours and times of stress. Regardless of how hard you work, there will be losses with the victories, so you must be able to work the hours, handle the stress, and take the losses in stride.

Based on current trends, many advocates see the legislative arena as one of the key places that the animal protection debate will be played out. Voter ballot initiatives are already changing the rules in factory farming where litigation failed. These initiatives, along with public sentiment, are not lost on legislators who will be receptive to information and education regarding animal law issues. For example, the deplorable conditions in some commercial breeding facilities, know as puppy mills, have already prompted voters and legislators to act in a number of states to mandate minimal care and treatment of breeding dogs.

In response, as the animal welfare movement has gained traction and public support, opposition is building. Agricultural producers that engage in Concentrated Animal Feeding Operations (CAFOs), hunting organizations, and commercial breeders who are the targets of animal welfare legislation are lobbying aggressively as well. Activity has increased, and is likely to continue to increase as the debate heats up on both sides of the issue.

If working as a lobbyist sounds like the right job for you, the next step is to decide whether to become an independent lobbyist, look for a position at a firm, or search for an in-house opportunity. If you have the expertise to be an independent lobbyist, you will need to determine what laws and regulations will apply to your practice and how to comply. There are various legal requirements for lobbyists in your state or with the federal government, such as registration and financial disclosures. Once in legal and ethical compliance, you are ready to set up your business and look for clients.

To pursue a career with a firm or as an in-house lobbyist will take a bit more research and effort, but that is where tenacity and social skills, the same skills needed to be a successful lobbyist, come into play. One place to start for education and information is the American League of Lobbyists, the industry's professional organization. It represents public affairs and government relations professionals and provides various resources, including training.

The Nonprofit World

If you are inspired by the work of the humane organizations in this book or a rescue group in your neighborhood, perhaps the nonprofit route is the career path for you. As covered in the "For-Profits and Nonprofits" section in Chapter 5, a nonprofit is an organization that is tax exempt under section 501(c)(3) of the Internal Revenue Code. It means the group was formed for a religious, charitable, scientific, literary, and/or educational purpose as defined by the IRS.

While the federal laws and regulations governing nonprofits are complex, the logistics of forming a nonprofit organization are not. It requires state and federal filings, but there is an abundance of free information available on state and federal websites, as well as numerous good books on the subject. The IRS has extensive information available at no cost on their website. There are also law firms that specialize in representing nonprofit organizations. Generally, the organizer files the necessary documents to set up a nonprofit corporation in the state where it plans to conduct business and/or where the organization is located. Each state has its own laws and requirements separate and apart from the federal requirements. Once the state requirements are met, the organization files the necessary documents to be granted 501(c)(3) status.

The real challenge is not in setting up the organization, but in everything else. First, you must decide whether there is a need for the services you plan to offer. As of April 2010, the National Center for Charitable Statistics reported there were 18,553 animal-related charities in the United States. Do you have a new idea? Also, it can take years of hard work to bring the organization to a level of credibility and financial security. It must be a labor of love or a passion, not one of financial gain.

Consider the following if you are thinking about starting a nonprofit.

- Will the goals and objectives of the organization qualify for nonprofit status? Make sure that your organization will meet the requirements.
- Is there saturation in the field in which you are interested? Are other organizations out there doing the same thing,

competing for the same donations and grants? How will you distinguish what you do?

- Do you have a business plan? Have you thought carefully about the program and developed a plan to help ensure your success?
- How do you plan to deliver the services? How many people do you need? How much money?
- Do you have support? How many people are willing to help you, not only with the management tasks, but the physical labor that may be required? You may find people willing to manage, but not roll up their sleeves. And you may find people who are willing to roll up their sleeves, but have so many other obligations that they simply do not have the time.
- How much expertise do you bring to the table, and at what point will it be necessary to hire someone? There are budgeting issues, financial reports, and disclosures to be considered that may require hiring an accountant.
- If you do not have a major donor going into the program, do you have the resources to start and fund these services or have them donated before you raise money?
- How much time do you have? If you do not have the financial wherewithal to support yourself while you build the organization, can you handle the responsibility while working another day job? Do you have someone to support you?
- Do you understand fundraising? Have you targeted possible grants? Do you know potential large donors who would be interested in supporting your organization?

Of course, the preceding questions and concerns do not factor in the rewards of doing good work. The benefits that come with doing charitable work for animals are personal. For many it's a labor of love that cannot be equaled.

If starting, building, and running a nonprofit is more work than you want to take on, consider looking for a position managing an animal-related nonprofit organization or joining up in some capacity with an existing organization. Medium and large organizations usually have executive directors or legal positions. A legal background would be a valuable asset in either position.

When we think of nonprofits, we tend to think of the large humane organizations, which are covered in Chapter 5, or the very small, financially struggling animal rescue groups. But there are numerous charitable organizations in between that have the resources to pay employees such as executive directors and staff attorneys. And if they do not have the financial resources, consider raising the money to pay your salary. Many executive directors are responsible for fundraising, which includes securing a grant or funding to pay their salaries.

Public Service

Federal and state legislators impact the lives of many people (and animals) through their power to make laws and influence public policy. Even at the local level, city officials pass ordinances that determine our legal rights and obligations regarding animals.

Many elected officials are lawyers. A law license is not required, but experience and education in the law are invaluable tools in understanding the political process and in drafting and comprehending legislation.

There are certain individuals who are destined for careers in public service. They enjoy the campaigning and election processes and find great satisfaction in working to improve the lives of U.S. citizens. Senfronia Thompson is one such individual. Her career profile shows how as a lawyer and public servant she is working to make life better for the "underdog," literally and figuratively.

Career Profile

Senfronia Thompson, Lawyer and State Representative
Texas House of Representatives
Austin and Houston, Texas

Ms. Senfronia Thompson is a lawyer and representative for District 141 in the Texas House of Representatives. A Houston resident, she began her career as a school-

teacher with the Houston Independent School District. In 1972, inspired by Barbara Jordan's election to the U.S. House of Representatives, Ms. Thompson launched her own campaign, won the election, and in 1973 took office to serve Northeast Houston and Humble. As she concludes her twentieth term, she has served longer in the Texas legislature than any other woman or African-American in Texas history—and she has not been sitting quietly on the sidelines.

Throughout her tenure, Ms. Thompson has taken on tough legislative issues and is well known for her efforts to fight discrimination against minorities, women, the elderly, and children. She has authored and passed more than 200 laws, including the James Byrd, Jr. Hate Crimes Act, laws prohibiting racial profiling, the Sexual Assault Program Fund, and scores of other reforms benefitting victims of discrimination and raising awareness of the issues.

Most recently, she has taken up the fight against animal cruelty, and in 2009, she introduced a commercial breeder bill to stop puppy mill cruelty. While the bill didn't pass, Ms. Thompson refused to give up and brought the bill back—successfully in 2011—with majority support that crossed party lines.

When asked how she decides to take on an issue, she said, "I have to feel for it. I am particularly compelled to act when I see an important issue that no one else will champion." In the case of puppy mills, she saw news stories with horrific scenes of dogs being abused and neglected, and no one was stepping up to address it. She adds, "When no one steps up, that issue is speaking directly to me and I will answer."

When she is not serving in the legislature, Ms. Thompson works as a lawyer in a Houston law firm. When in session, no two days are the same. She spends her days dealing with the issues and the players, as well as developing strategies to further her agenda. Ms. Thompson is quick to note that politics is a demanding field, requiring lawmakers to address the needs of their constituents, the public, and their fellow legislators, all the while staying true to their personal principles.

What does it take to succeed in public service? First, it takes confidence in the fact that you are qualified and can succeed. Ms. Thompson advises those thinking about public service to be willing to give of yourself and work to make a contribution to society, not just for today but for the future. Short-term successes and fleeting awards will not sustain you over the long haul. And as for credentials beyond the law degree, Ms. Thompson unequivocally believes that common sense and compassion are the two most important traits. Through her many years of public service and recent efforts to end animal cruelty, she has proven that she has both.

7 Animal Protection and Pro Bono

A book about careers in animal law would not be complete without a discussion of the role of pro bono legal services in advancing the field, furthering the cause of animal protection, and generating careers. Many animal lawyers have spent most or significant parts of their working lives volunteering or working for reduced compensation on behalf of animals. For some, their efforts have led to paying jobs and for others, volunteering has been an end in itself. For all, however, their work comes from a personal commitment to the worth of animals and the fact that, as lawyers, they have a "special responsibility for the quality of justice," as stated in the Preamble to the ABA Model Rules of Professional Responsibility.

As in other social justice movements, such as civil rights, environmental protection, and women's rights, lawyers have seen societal "wrongs" that they can and want to "right" through their legal knowledge and expertise. In the beginning, the battles are usually fought on shoestring or nonexistent budgets with a few committed lawyers donating their time, resources, and more until others join the movement.

Animal protection has followed a similar path, and there continues to be a significant need for lawyers willing to donate their time and energy to the movement.

You may have decided that, given your own situation, a career in animal law will not work for you. But you may have also found animal law to be interesting and challenging and a way to fulfill your own need to make a difference. Through pro bono services you can work to protect animals, give back to the community, and hone your legal skills.

All lawyers are urged by their firms and professional organizations to volunteer their time. Volunteering is usually defined as helping humans, but the need is particularly relevant in animal law cases. The *de facto* clients, the animals, will never be able to pay, and they are often at the bottom of the priority list given their legal status as property.

As you read earlier, fighting animal cruelty through the legal system gathered steam in the early 1980s when a group of lawyers across the country started talking to each other about the injustices they saw. These lawyers did not stop with talking, and donated their time to mount legal challenges against what they saw as lax enforcement of animal protection laws and to raise awareness of the issues. Their work was challenging. They sued for enforcement of current animal protection laws and often lost based on lack of standing.

But these lawyers did not give up, and over the years have achieved success on several fronts. More importantly, they set a standard for new lawyers to take on the challenges and rewards of animal cases. Volunteerism continues to play a key role in advancing animal welfare, locally and nationally, as more law firms are taking on pro bono causes for animals.

If you are in a firm, you can ask to have your pro bono hours in the area of animal welfare. At one time there was resistant to allowing "non-human" volunteer work, but that is changing. The opportunities vary and you can choose the types of cases and work you want to do. In addition to helping animals, you can gain valuable legal knowledge through trial work, brief writing, and research on constitutional issues.

If you are interested, but wondering how you can work another case into your schedule, read on.

On a National Level

Career Profile

David J. Wolfson, Partner
Milbank, Tweed, Hadley & McCloy LLP
New York, New York

David Wolfson is a partner in the Global Corporate Group at Milbank, Tweed, Hadley & McCloy LLP, an international law firm with eleven offices throughout the United States and around the world. David received his bachelor's degree from Duke University, his Common Professional Examination Postgraduate Diploma in Law from the College of Law, London, England, and his juris doctor from Columbia School of Law, where he was a Harlan Fiske Stone Scholar.

Working out of his firm's New York office, David represents international and domestic companies in business matters including mergers and acquisitions, private equity and venture capital investments, joint ventures, and corporate restructurings. Add to that a long-standing commitment to animal protection, particularly farm animals, that includes pro bono work for the Humane Society of the United States and Farm Sanctuary; extensive writings on animal protection issues; active involvement in all levels of regulatory and legislative issues; and teaching positions in animal law at Columbia Law School, Harvard Law School, New York University School of Law, Cardozo Law School, and Yale Law School. Finally, add to those credentials his unfailing willingness to say "yes" to a request when it means he can help animals.

David began his pro bono work in animal welfare while still in law school, volunteering with the American Society for the Prevention of Cruelty to Animals (ASPCA) and Farm Sanctuary. Unlike some of the other lawyers profiled in this book, he knew early on that animal protection work would always be part of his law practice, although perhaps not the significant part it has actually played through the years. When he joined Milbank, Tweed, Hadley & McCloy in 1993 he brought his pro bono client, Farm Sanctuary, with him. David's firm supported his pro bono work in animal law when he joined as an associate at a time when animal law was still new and uncharted territory. The firm continues to support his work today as a partner. So do not be reluctant to approach your firm about pro bono work in animal law. Do not assume the answer will be no. Today there is a great deal of public and legal industry support for taking animal law cases.

After almost twenty years of handling virtually every type of animal case, David spends most of his pro bono time as a consultant, working with various animal protection organizations on planning and legal strategies. His years of experience are invaluable, particularly to new organizations and lawyers who have yet to learn the complex animal law landscape. When asked how he has managed to handle the demands of pro bono cases and the demands of becoming a partner at a large international law firm, he simply says it was not hard to juggle, adding that "a pro bono case simply became another stack on my desk, another client."

When looking at pro bono opportunities, consider the fact that animal cases cover many areas: companion animals, farm animals, marine mammals, and wild animals, to name a few. In choosing an area in which to work, David advises choosing based on what you care about most. In choosing clients, start working with nonprofit organizations rather than individuals, as individual cases can be more difficult. Find the organizations that match your interests. From there, it's simply a matter of getting involved. Whether you are looking for pro bono work or paying clients, it is about relationships. Attend animal-related conferences and legal conferences and meet the people in these organizations. Tell them you want to work for them and eventually the work will come. Be patient and continue to build relationships with those people who share your interests. Volunteer to help in nonlegal areas as well.

When you take a case, start with a small project that will not require you to litigate. As you have learned if you have read the previous pages of this book, animal law is complex. Litigation can be complicated and time consuming. A contracts or nonprofit matter will allow you to start slowly, complete a successful project, and help you gain experience and confidence to take on some of the tougher cases later on.

The rewards of volunteering are as varied as the people who do it. David had been interested in legal issues related to animals since law school. Once he graduated and started taking cases, he realized that he was at the beginning of a social justice movement, which was very exciting. His contributions to a still nascent animal protection movement came during a time of increased activity, which proved to be a turning point in many areas. Several law schools launched animal law journals, and a seminal animal law conference, which David co-organized, was held in New York City to a standing-room-only crowd. The legal community, the public, and animal-related businesses and organizations began to take notice.

Since that time animal law and the animal protection movement have advanced. Students are taking animal law classes with the intention of practicing in the field, lawyers who are litigating and advancing animal issues have increased in number and have become more sophisticated in their efforts, and the public is becoming increasingly more educated in animal protection issues. In the future, volunteer lawyers will play key roles in moving the animal protection movement into the next phase. While litigation is still an important tool for furthering change, nonprofits are reassessing their strategies and choosing their battles carefully. Some organizations are finding that success means taking on smaller, but winnable, battles and fewer big lawsuits that have fewer chances of success. David sees a future focused increasingly on legislative issues and regulations. The sought-after volunteers will have experience in administrative and constitutional law.

Making a Difference in Your Community

David Wolfson's story is one that is national, even international, in scope. For most lawyers who work in smaller firms or reside in cities other than New York, David's pro bono activities in animal protection may seem out of reach. So how do you find pro bono animal cases in your own community and fit them into your schedule, in addition to the responsibilities of a job and family? Randy Turner has the answer, and in commitment to volunteerism and animal protection, there is only one factor—location—that distinguishes Randy Turner from David Wolfson.

Career Profile

Randy Turner, Partner
Turner & McKenzie, P.C
Fort Worth, Texas

Randy Turner lives in Fort Worth, Texas, and has spent his almost thirty-year career in a solo or small practice setting. He graduated from St. Mary's School of Law in San Antonio and is currently a partner with Turner and McKenzie, P.C., a three-lawyer firm that specializes in personal injury, criminal law, and animal law. He is board certified by the Texas Board of Legal Specialization in personal injury and civil trial law. As a partner he is responsible for new business development, handling cases, and assisting in the management of the firm. In addition to his paying clients, there is always a steady stream of pro bono animal cases that keeps him busy.

Randy's pro bono work began shortly after he graduated from law school. Animal law was not a recognized field of practice in 1980, so he simply called humane organizations and volunteered to help. They welcomed his offer, and he subsequently served on the boards of many organizations. As word of Randy's legal expertise and commitment to animal protection grew, so did his caseload. Over the past thirty years Randy has litigated many cases on a pro bono or reduced-fee basis including the defense of animal rights activists, dangerous dog hearings, and veterinary malpractice. He has represented individuals in claims against pet shops, dog breeders, and puppy mills and defended rescue groups and humane organizations. He has sued local and state governments when they have passed unconstitutional laws and local ordinances or when law enforcement has overstepped its constitutional boundaries.

In addition to his local work, Randy is also involved in international wildlife conservation efforts. Believing that the loss of an endangered species is a loss to everyone, he has volunteered in orangutan rehabilitation in Borneo, elephant conservation in Kenya, and black rhino conservation in Zimbabwe.

Today, Randy continues his work in animal protection. In Texas, a large state with many rural areas, there is no shortage of people and animals in need. Poverty, lack of education, sketchy enforcement of animal cruelty laws, and the recent hysteria regarding dangerous dogs have resulted in unnecessary euthanasia and the separation of beloved companion animals from owners who did not have legal representation.

When asked how he manages a small firm, travels the world, and handles pro bono cases, he admits, "It's hard sometimes, but I can't see an injustice and just sit back and allow it to happen. I am passionate about animal protection and I simply view it as part of my work as a lawyer. When I have a particularly heavy workload, I usually work on my pro bono cases on the weekends."

Animal law has changed since Randy took his first case. However, although the field has grown, the number of lawyers taking on individual cases has not. While small, these cases are sometimes complex legally and even experienced lawyers may need guidance that is not always available. Randy sees a great need in Texas for lawyers, particularly in smaller jurisdictions, who will devote even a small number of pro bono hours to animal protection, as well as for experienced animal lawyers to mentor them. He hopes to see more programs to raise awareness and develop and mentor lawyers interested in taking cases in the future.

As for personal aspirations, Randy looks at every case as an opportunity to advance the law. Texas is still bound by nineteenth-century precedent on animal valuation, and Randy is intent on seeing this antiquated precedent replaced with a twenty-first century case. And if that is too slow in coming, he is also working on the legislative side to pass laws that promote animal welfare in Texas.

"Although they are mostly pro bono, my animal law cases are by far the most rewarding part of my law practice."

Conclusion

8

Trends in Animal Law

Part of this book consists of interviews with lawyers who are working in various areas of animal law and related fields. One of the questions I asked was what trends they were seeing in animal law and animal welfare. Based on their answers and my own experience, the following are the trends we think will shape the field of animal law and future careers.

Legislation

- An increasing amount of animal-related legislation, both pro- and anti-animal, is being introduced and passed at the local, state, national, and international levels. Most recently, particular attention has been paid to two main areas: (1) strengthening protections for companion animals—such as stricter regulation of commercial breeders, felony anti-dog fighting measures, and increased penalties for animal cruelty; and (2) improving the welfare of farm animals—either directly through a series of high-profile, state public ballot initiatives or direct legislative action.

Litigation

- Litigation also remains an active strategy to promote animal welfare, as humane organizations, pro-animal law firms, and other animal protection groups continue filing suits to enforce animal laws at all available levels of redress. These organizations constantly monitor the legal landscape and have become more creative and better prepared in fashioning and winning suits that benefit the well-being and status of animals. Animal lawyers report seeing an evolution in the types of litigation being initiated. Lawyers see constitutional issues playing a more prominent role in future litigation. While it was a case involving the First Amendment, *U.S. v. Stevens*, heard by the U.S. Supreme Court in 2009, was also about animal cruelty. It was a seminal case for animal law in that issues regarding animal cruelty and whether animals warranted special protection under the U.S. Constitution were actually discussed in the opinion. The case was argued in part for greater protection for animals that were being abused in a form of pornography called "crush videos."
- The amount of individual litigation continues to rise as people sue to recover for the injury or death of their animals despite the lack of adequate damages. As pressure mounts to award greater damages for the death of a companion animal, this will be an area to watch.

Academia

- On the academic front, there has been an exponential increase in the interest and acceptance of animal law as a distinct discipline by law schools and law students. In the past decade the number of law schools offering animal law classes has increased ten-fold. In addition, animal studies as a field is generally growing at the undergraduate and graduate levels, with New York University recently announcing a minor in animal studies.
- Animal law classes continue to be popular as students take classes with an interest in practicing in the field when they graduate. Students also may look for law schools with an animal law curriculum.

The Legal Profession

- At the professional level, state and local bar associations continue to add animal law sections and offer animal law-related CLE programs. In 2004, the ABA Tort Trial and Insurance Practice Section established an Animal Law Committee that has had constant growth in membership and has been active in publishing books and other publications, hosting educational symposia, and drafting model legislation and policy recommendations.

The Public

- There is a growing public interest in and awareness of animal welfare issues. Books about animals are being published by mainstream publishers on topics from factory farming to the lives of dogs; films and television programs devoted to animals are popular and continue to expand. The public's fascination with animals is showing no signs of diminishing.
- States, cities and counties are devoting increased resources to animal cruelty prosecutions, armed with mounting empirical evidence of the link between animal abuse and human violence. Many departments now include animal crime education in their standard police training, and some jurisdictions have created stand-alone animal cruelty divisions with dedicated prosecutors, law enforcement personnel, and advanced resource sharing among agencies. Veterinary forensics is also emerging as a discipline unto itself to assist in animal cruelty, dog bite, and breed ban cases.
- There is increasing public awareness, locally and internationally, regarding factory farming's drain on the world's natural resources and its consequential environmental damage.

It is impossible to predict what the future will hold for our relationship with animals. For law students and animal lawyers, the next phase of animal law will consist of different challenges and opportunities. What is certain, however, is that lawyers will help shape that future. Science and technology, population growth, environmental issues, and greater wealth in developing countries are just a few factors that have implications for animals and the law.

While much has been accomplished, much remains to be done in order to elevate animal law to the position of other legal disciplines. Positive steps toward that end include animal law class at all law schools; more law firms that offer animal law as an area of expertise; legislation that adequately addresses the unique status of animals; and expansive legal scholarship that educates, advances discourse, and shapes opinions.

Animal law will continue its evolution thanks to the contributions of the people who care about animals and the law. For those not yet under the influence of animal law's intellectual, social, and legal appeal, I hope this book has enticed you.

Appendix

A

Select Bibliography

The following is a select bibliography of works consulted in the writing of this book and in the development of my animal law practice. It is by no means a complete list of the relevant works in the field of animal law and animal protection. I have included some books due to their significant and lasting contributions to the animal protection movement, and others based on their legal guidance and career advice.

TAIMIE L. BRYANT, REBECCA HUSS, & DAVID N. CASSUTO, ANIMAL LAW AND THE COURTS: A READER (THOMSON/WEST, 2008).

DAVID FAVRE, ANIMAL LAW: WELFARE, INTERESTS, AND RIGHTS (2nd ed., Aspen Publishers, 2011).

JAY G FOONBERG, HOW TO START & BUILD A LAW PRACTICE (5th ed., ABA Law Practice Management Section, 2004).

GARY L. FRANCIONE, ANIMALS, PROPERTY, AND THE LAW (Temple University Press, 1995).

TOM REGEN, THE CASE FOR ANIMAL RIGHTS (University of California Press, 2004).

BERNARD E. ROLLIN, ANIMAL RIGHTS & HUMAN MORALITY (3d ed., Prometheus Books, 2006).

JOAN E. SCHAFFNER, ED., THE LAWYER'S GUIDE TO DANGEROUS DOG ISSUES (ABA Publishing, 2009).

JOAN E. SCHAFFNER, AN INTRODUCTION TO ANIMALS AND THE LAW (Palgrave Macmillan, 2011).

PETER SINGER, ANIMAL LIBERATION (HarperCollins, 2002).

CASS R. SUNSTEIN & MARTHA C. NUSSBAUM, EDS., ANIMAL RIGHTS: CURRENT DEBATES AND NEW DIRECTIONS (Oxford University Press, 2004).

KAROL TAYLOR & JANET M. RUCK, GUIDE TO AMERICA'S FEDERAL JOBS (4th ed., JIST Publishing, 2009).

BRUCE A. WAGMAN, SONIA S. WAISMAN, & PAMELA D. FRASCH, ANIMAL LAW: CASES AND MATERIALS (4th ed., Carolina Academic Press, 2010).

STEVEN M. WISE, RATTLING THE CAGE: TOWARD LEGAL RIGHTS FOR ANIMALS (Perseus Books, 2000).

Appendix

B

Resources

The following is a list of resources that were either mentioned in the book or provide further information on animal law and careers.

Organizations, Companies, and Universities

American Bar Association Tort Trial and Insurance Practice Section Animal Law Committee
http://apps.americanbar.org/dch/committee.cfm?com=IL201050

American Bar Association Business Law Section/Nonprofit Organizations
http://apps.americanbar.org/dch/committee.cfm?com=CL580000

The American League of Lobbyists
http://www.alldc.org

Animal Legal Defense Fund
http://www.aldf.org

Animal People (Newspaper)
http://www.animalpeoplenews.org

Animal and Plant Health Inspection Service
http://www.aphis.usda.gov

Professor Gerry W. Beyer, Texas Tech University School of Law
Estate Planning for Pets
http://www.professorbeyer.com

Center for Animal Law Studies at Lewis & Clark in collaboration with the Animal Legal Defense Fund
http://www.lclark.edu/law/centers/animal_law_studies

Congressional Research Service
http://www.loc.gov/crsinfo

Digital Text Platform Publishing
http://www.amazon.com

George Washington University Law School
http://www.law.gwu.edu

Internal Revenue Service: Charities and Nonprofits
http://www.irs.gov/charities

International Animal-Law
http://www.animal-law.biz

Michigan State University College of Law: Animal Legal and Historical Center
http://www.animallaw.info

The National Center for Charitable Statistics
http://nccs.urban.org

The National Geographic Channel Program Ideas
https://www.ngcideas.com

The Niman Ranch
http://www.nimanranch.com

PetSmart Careers
http://careers.petsmart.com

United States Department of Agriculture
http://usda.gov

United States Department of Homeland Security
http://www.dhs.gov

United States Department of the Interior
http://www.doi.gov

United States Department of Interior Bureau of Land Management
http://www.blm.gov

United States Department of Justice Job Site
http://www.justice.gov/oarm

United States Department of Justice Student Opportunities
http://www.justice.gov/careers/student-opportunities.html

United States Environmental Protection Agency
http://www.epa.gov

United States Government
http://www.usa.gov

United States Office of Personnel Management Jobs Site
http://www.usajobs.gov

Animal Law Journals

Animal Law
Lewis & Clark Law School
http://law.lclark.edu/law_reviews/animal_law_review/

Journal of Animal Law
Michigan State University College of Law
http://www.animallaw.info/policy/pojouranimlawinfo.htm

Stanford Journal of Animal Law and Policy
Stanford Law School
http://sjalp.stanford.edu

State Animal Law Sections and Committees

The following state bar associations have animal law sections or committees. The state bar's main website address is listed where no specific animal law web page was found.

Arizona
Arizona Bar Animal Law Section
http://www.azbar.org

Connecticut
Connecticut Bar Animal Law Committee
https://www.ctbar.org/Sections%20Committees/Committees/AnimalLaw.aspx

Florida
Florida Bar Animal Law Committee
http://www.floridabar.org

Georgia
Animal Law Bar Section Georgia
http://www.gabar.org/sections/section_web_pages/animal_law

Illinois
Illinois State Bar Association Animal Law Section
http://www.isba.org/sections/animallaw

Indiana
Indiana State Bar Association Animal Law Committee
http://www.inbar.org/ISBALinks/Committees/AnimalLaw/tabid/334/Default.aspx

Louisiana
Louisiana State Bar Animal Law Section
http://www.animallawla.org/index.htm

Maryland
Maryland State Bar Animal Law Section
http://www.msba.org/sec_comm/sections/animallaw

Massachusetts
Massachusetts Bar Association's Animal Law Practice Group
http://www.massbar.org/publications/lawyers-journal/2008/may/animal-law-practice-group-draws-large-crowd-for-first-meeting

Michigan
State Bar of Michigan Animal Law Section
http://www.michbar.org/animal

Minnesota
Animal Law Section of the Minnesota State Bar Association
http://www2.mnbar.org/sections/animal-law

Missouri
Missouri Bar Animal Law Committee
http://www.mobar.org/3e20fee3-d24b-4bf4-a5e4-954e01b92218.aspx

New Jersey
New Jersey State Bar Association Animal Law Committee
http://www.njsba.com/committees_sections/special/animal.cfm

New York
New York State Bar Association Special Committee on Animals and the Law
http://www.nysba.org/AM/Template.cfm?Section=Committee_on_Animals_and_the_Law_Home

Oregon
Oregon Animal Law Section
http://www.oregonanimallaw.com

Pennsylvania
Pennsylvania Bar Animal Law Committee
http://www.pabar.org/public/committees/animal

Texas
State Bar of Texas Animal Law Section
http://www.animallawsection.org

Washington
Washington Bar Animal Law Section
http://www.wsba.org/lawyers/groups/animallaw/default1.htm

Appendix

C

Nonprofit Organizations

The following nonprofits represent a small sample of the more than 18,000 animal-related charities in the United States. This list is for informational purposes only; it is intended to give the reader a sense of the diversity and scope of organizations that deal with animal issues. This list is not all-inclusive, nor does the presence of an organization on the list reflect any endorsement of the activities of the organization.

African Wildlife Foundation
http://www.awf.org

Alley Cat Allies
http://www.alleycat.org

Alliance for Contraception of Cats and Dogs
http://www.acc-d.org

Alternatives for Research and Development Foundation
http://www.ardf-online.org

American Anti-Vivisection Society
http://www.aavs.org

American Eagle Foundation
http://www.eagles.org

American Humane Association
http://www.americanhumane.org/

American Society for the Prevention of Cruelty to Animals
http://www.aspca.org

Animal Acres
http://www.animalacres.org

Animal Defenders International
http://www.ad-international.org/adi_world

Animal Legal Defense Fund
http://www.aldf.org

Assistance Dog United Campaign
http://www.assistancedogunitedcampaign.org

Best Friends Animal Sanctuary
http://www.bestfriends.org

Bidawee Home Association
http://www.bideawee.org

Big Cat Rescue
http://www.bigcatrescue.org

Born Free USA
http://www.bornfreeusa.org

Buffalo Field Campaign
http://www.buffalofieldcampaign.org

Canine Assistants
http://www.canineassistants.org

Compassion Over Killing
http://www.cok.net

Days End Farm Horse Rescue
http://www.defhr.org

Defenders of Wildlife
http://www.defenders.org

DELTA Rescue
http://www.deltarescue.org

Dian Fossey Gorilla Fund International
http://gorillafund.org

DJT Foundation
http://www.djtfoundation.org

Dogs Deserve Better
http://www.dogsdeservebetter.com

Elephant Sanctuary in Tennessee
http://www.elephants.com

Environmental Defense Fund
http://www.edf.org

Farm for Animals
http://www.farmusa.org

Farm Sanctuary
http://www.farmsanctuary.org

Food Animal Concerns Trust
http://www.foodanimalconcerns.org

Friends of Animals
http://www.friendsofanimals.org

Front Range Equine Rescue
http://www.frontrangeequinerescue.org

Fund for Animals
http://www.fundforanimals.org

Gorilla Foundation
http://www.koko.org

Greenpeace & Greenpeace Fund
http://www.greenpeace.org

Grey 2K USA Education Fund
http://www.grey2kusaedu.org

Guide Dogs for the Blind, Inc.
http://www.guidedogs.com

Guide Dogs of America
http://www.guidedogsofamerica.org

Hearts United for Animals
http://www.hua.org

Helen Woodward Animal Center
http://www.animalcenter.org

Humane Farming Association
http://www.hfa.org

The Humane Society of the United States
http://www.humanesociety.org

In Defense of Animals
http://www.idausa.org

International Exotic Feline Sanctuary
http://www.bigcat.org

International Fund for Animal Welfare
http://www.ifaw.org

International Primate Protection League
http://www.ippl.org

International Society for Animal Rights
http://www.isaronline.org/index.html

Jane Goodall Institute
http://www.janegoodall.org

Kinship Circle
http://www.kinshipcircle.org

Last Chance for Animals
http://www.lcanimal.org

Lawyers in Defense of Animals
http://www.njlida.org

Lifesavers Wild Horse Rescue
http://www.wildhorserescue.org

Maddie's Fund
http://www.maddiesfund.org

Marine Mammal Center
http://www.marinemammalcenter.org

Mercy for Animals
http://www.mercyforanimals.org

Metroplex Animal Coaltion
http://www.metroplexanimalcoalition.org

Millan Foundation
http://www.millanfoundation.org

National Anti-Vivisection Society
http://www.navs.org

National Audubon Society
http://www.audubon.org

National Greyhound Foundation
http://www.4greyhounds.org

National Institute for Animal Advocacy
http://www.nifaa.org

National Wildlife Federation
http://www.nwf.org

National Resources Defense Council
http://www.nrdc.org

The Nature Conservancy
http://www.nature.org

NEADS: Dogs for Deaf and Disabled Americans
http://www.neads.org

Neighborhood Cats
http://www.neighborhoodcats.org

Noah's Lost Ark
http://www.noahslostark.org

Noah's Wish
http://www.noahswish.org

Orangutan Foundation International
http://www.orangutan.org

Our Hen House
http://www.ourhenhouse.org

Paws with a Cause
http://www.pawswithacause.org

Peaceful Donkey Rescue
http://donkeyrescue.donordrive.com

People for the Ethical Treatment of Animals
http://www.peta.org

People Helping Horses
http://peoplehelpinghorses.org

Peregrine Fund
http://www.peregrinefund.org

Performing Animal Welfare Society
http://www.pawsweb.org

PetSmart Charities
http://www.petsmartcharities.org

Physicians Committee for Responsible Medicine
http://www.pcrm.org

Redwings Horse Sanctuary
http://redwingshorsesanctuary.org

Release Chimpanzees
http://www.releasechimps.org

Sea Shepherd Conservation Society
http://www.seashepherd.org

Search Dog Foundation, National Disaster
http://www.searchdogfoundation.org

Seeing Eye, Inc.
http://www.seeingeye.org

Showing Animals Respect and Kindness
http://sharkonline.org

Sierra Club
http://www.sierraclub.org

Six Hundred Million Stray Dogs Need You
http://www.600millionstraydogs.com

Species Survival Network
http://www.ssn.org

SPCA International
http://www.spcai.org

Support Dogs, Inc.
http://www.supportdogs.org

Tiger Creek Wildlife Refuge
http://www.tigercreek.org

Tiger Haven
http://www.tigerhaven.org

United Animal Nations
http://www.uan.org

United Poultry Concerns
http://www.upc-online.org

Wild Burro Rescue
http://www.wildburrorescue.org

Wild Earth Guardians
http://www.wildearthguardians.org

Wilderness Society
http://wilderness.org

Wildlife Conservation Society
http://www.wcs.org

Wildlife Waystation
http://wildlifewaystation.org

World Society for the Protection of Animals
http://www.wspa-international.org

World Wildlife Fund
http://www.worldwildlife.org

Worldwatch Institute
http://www.worldwatch.org

Index

iPad in One Hour for Lawyers
By Tom Mighell
Whether you are a new or a more advanced iPad user, *iPad in One Hour for Lawyers* takes a great deal of the mystery and confusion out of using your iPad. Ideal for lawyers who want to get up to speed swiftly, this book presents the essentials so you don't get bogged down in technical jargon and extraneous features and apps. In just six, short lessons, you'll learn how to:

- Quickly Navigate and Use the iPad User Interface
- Set Up Mail, Calendar, and Contacts
- Create and Use Folders to Multitask and Manage Apps
- Add Files to Your iPad, and Sync Them
- View and Manage Pleadings, Case Law, Contracts, and other Legal Documents
- Use Your iPad to Take Notes and Create Documents
- Use Legal-Specific Apps at Trial or in Doing Research

The Lawyer's Guide to Marketing Your Practice, Second Edition
Edited by James A. Durham and Deborah McMurray
This book is packed with practical ideas, innovative strategies, useful checklists, and sample marketing and action plans to help you implement a successful, multi-faceted, and profit-enhancing marketing plan for your firm. Organized into four sections, this illuminating resource covers: Developing Your Approach; Enhancing Your Image; Implementing Marketing Strategies and Maintaining Your Program. Appendix materials include an instructive primer on market research to inform you on research methodologies that support the marketing of legal services. The accompanying CD-ROM contains a wealth of checklists, plans, and other sample reports, questionnaires, and templates—all designed to make implementing your marketing strategy as easy as possible!

Nonlegal Careers for Lawyers, Fifth Edition
By William D. Henslee, Gary A. Munneke, Ellen Wayne
Perhaps you are a law student who realizes that practicing law is not what you want to do. Or maybe you are a practicing lawyer who no longer feels satisfied with your work. If you feel it's time for a change, this newly revised guidebook will show you what you can do with your law degree, besides practice law. More importantly, this book will illustrate how to use your legal skills to rise above the competition.

How to Start and Build a Law Practice, Platinum Fifth Edition
By Jay G Foonberg
This classic ABA bestseller has been used by tens of thousands of lawyers as the comprehensive guide to planning, launching, and growing a successful practice. It's packed with over 600 pages of guidance on identifying the right location, finding clients, setting fees, managing your office, maintaining an ethical and responsible practice, maximizing available resources, upholding your standards, and much more. You'll find the information you need to successfully launch your practice, run it at maximum efficiency, and avoid potential pitfalls along the way. If you're committed to starting—and growing—your own practice, this one book will give you the expert advice you need to make it succeed for years to come.

Job Quest for Lawyers
By Sheila Nielsen
Job Quest for Lawyers provides step-by-step guidance that finally makes networking inspiring instead of a chore. The "quest" motif applies to each stage of the job search, and is used to help readers understand how to create a positive and effective networking experience. The book demystifies networking by including illustrations from the author's own experiences and from the stories of her clients that provide examples of the real world do's and don'ts of how to conduct a productive job search. Unlike so many other career books, *Job Quest for Lawyers* is a process-focused book that is eminently applicable to attorneys at all phases of their careers, from new graduates to senior lawyers. Lawyers at all stages of practice will benefit from reading this book.

The Busy Lawyer's Guide to Success: Essential Tips to Power Your Practice
By Reid F. Trautz and Dan Pinnington
Busy lawyers do not have dozens of extra hours to conduct research looking for new tips and ideas to streamline and enhance their practice of law. They need "just-in-time" learning to acquire the knowledge necessary to build their practices. This convenient pocket guide is the "best ever" collection of practical tips, ideas, and techniques to help you survive, thrive, and find success in the practice of law.

30-Day Risk-Free Order Form

Call Today! 1-800-285-2221

Monday–Friday, 7:30 AM – 5:30 PM, Central Time

Qty	Title	LPM Price	Regular Price	Total
_____	The Legal Career Guide: From Law Student to Lawyer, Fifth Edition (5110479)	$ 29.95	$ 34.95	$_______
_____	Women-at-Law: Lessons Learned Along the Pathways to Success (5110509)	39.95	49.95	$_______
_____	The Lawyer's Guide to Balancing Life and Work, Second Edition (5110566)	29.95	39.95	$_______
_____	How to Build and Manage a Personal Injury Practice, Second Edition (5110575)	54.95	64.95	$_______
_____	The Lawyer's Guide to Governing Your Firm (5110684)	89.95	129.95	$_______
_____	How to Build and Manage an Estates Practice, Second Edition (5110421)	44.95	54.95	$_______
_____	iPadin One Hour for Lawyers (5110719)	19.95	34.95	$_______
_____	The Lawyer's Guide to Marketing Your Practice, Second Edition (5110500)	79.95	89.95	$_______
_____	Nonlegal Careers for Lawyers (5110567)	29.95	34.95	$_______
_____	How to Start and Build a Law Practice, Platinum Fifth Edition (5110508)	57.95	69.95	$_______
_____	Job Quest for Lawyers (5110725)	39.95	49.95	$_______
_____	The Busy Lawyer's Guide to Success: Essential Tips to Power Your Practice (5110687)	44.95	69.95	$_______

***Postage and Handling**

$10.00 to $49.99	$5.95
$50.00 to $99.99	$7.95
$100.00 to $199.99	$9.95
$200.00+	$12.95

****Tax**

DC residents add 6%

IL residents add 9.75%

***Postage and Handling** $_______

****Tax** $_______

TOTAL $_______

PAYMENT

❑ Check enclosed (to the ABA)

❑ Visa ❑ MasterCard ❑ American Express

Account Number Exp. Date Signature

Name Firm

Address

City State Zip

Phone Number E-Mail Address

Guarantee

If—for any reason—you are not satisfied with your purchase, you may return it within 30 days of receipt for a complete refund of the price of the book(s). No questions asked!

Mail: ABA Publication Orders, P.O. Box 10892, Chicago, Illinois 60610-0892 ♦ Phone: 1-800-285-2221 ♦ FAX: 312-988-5568

E-Mail: abasvcctr@americanbar.org ♦ Internet: http://www.lawpractice.org/catalog